# Bible Interpretations

Third Series

January 3 - March 27, 1892

*Isaiah 11:1-10 to Isaiah 40:1-10*

# Bible Interpretations

## Third Series

*Isaiah 11:1-10 to Isaiah 40:1-10*

These Bible Interpretations were given during the early eighteen nineties at the Christian Science Theological Seminary at Chicago, Illinois. This Seminary was independent of the First Church of Christ Scientist in Boston, Mass.

### By

### Emma Curtis Hopkins

*President of the Christian Science Theological Seminary at Chicago, Illinois*

WISEWOMAN PRESS

*Bible Interpretations: Third Series*

By Emma Curtis Hopkins


© WiseWoman Press

Managing Editor: Michael Terranova


ISBN: 978-0-945385-53-0


WiseWoman Press

Portland, OR 97217


www.wisewomanpress.com

www.emmacurtishopkins.com

# CONTENTS

|  |  |  |
|---|---|---|
|  | Foreword by Rev. Natalie R. Jean | vii |
|  | Introduction by Rev. Michael Terranova | ix |
| I. | A GOLDEN PROMISE | 1 |
|  | *Isaiah 11:1-10* |  |
| II. | THE TWELVE GATES | 13 |
|  | *Isaiah 26:1-10* |  |
| III. | WHO ARE DRUNKARDS | 23 |
|  | *Isaiah 28:1-13* |  |
| IV. | AWAKE THOU THAT SLEEPEST | 35 |
|  | *Isaiah 37:1-21* |  |
| V. | THE HEALING LIGHT | 47 |
|  | *Isaiah 53:1-12* |  |
| VI. | TRUE IDEAL OF GOD | 61 |
|  | *Isaiah 55:1-13* |  |
| VII. | HEAVEN AROUND US | 73 |
|  | *Jeremiah 31:14-37* |  |
| VIII. | BUT ONE SUBSTANCE | 85 |
|  | *Jeremiah 36:19-31* |  |
| IX. | JUSTICE OF JEHOVAH | 95 |
|  | *Jeremiah 37:11-21* |  |
| X. | GOD AND MAN ARE ONE | 107 |
|  | *Jeremiah 39:1-10* |  |
| XI. | SPIRITUAL IDEAS | 115 |
|  | *Ezekiel 4:9, 36:25-38* |  |
| XII. | ALL FLESH IS GRASS | 123 |
|  | *Isaiah 40:1-10* |  |
| XIII. | THE OLD AND THE NEW CONTRASTED | 133 |
|  | *REVIEW* |  |
|  | List of Bible Interpretation Series | 146 |

# Foreword

*By Rev. Natalie R. Jean*

I have read many teachings by Emma Curtis Hopkins, but the teachings that touch the very essence of my soul are her Bible Interpretations. There are many books written on the teachings of the Bible, but none can touch the surface of the true messages more than these Bible interpretations. With each word you can feel and see how Spirit spoke through Emma. The mystical interpretations take you on a wonderful journey to Self Realization.

Each passage opens your consciousness to a new awareness of the realities of life. The illusions of life seem to disappear through each interpretation. Emma teaches that we are the key that unlocks the doorway to the light that shines within. She incorporates ideals of other religions into her teachings, in order to understand the commonalities, so that there is a complete understanding of our Oneness. Emma opens our eyes and mind to a better today and exciting future.

Emma Curtis Hopkins, one of the Founders of New Thought teaches us to love ourselves, to speak our Truth, and to focus on our Good. My life has moved in wonderful directions because of her teachings. I know the only thing that can move me in this world is God. May these interpretations guide you to a similar path and may you truly remember that "There Is Good For You and You Ought to Have It."

# Introduction

Emma Curtis Hopkins was born in 1849 in Killingsly, Connecticut. She passed on April 8, 1925. Mrs. Hopkins had a marvelous education and could read many of the worlds classical texts in their original language. During her extensive studies she was always able to discover the Universal Truths in each of the world's sacred traditions. She quotes from many of these teachings in her writings. As she was a very private person, we know little about her personal life. What we do know has been gleaned from other people or from the archived writings we have been able to discover.

Emma Curtis Hopkins was one of the greatest influences on the New Thought movement in the United States. She taught over 50,000 people the Universal Truth of knowing "God is All there is." She taught many of founders of early New Thought, and in turn these individuals expanded the influence of her teachings. All of her writings encourage the student to enter into a personal relationship with God. She presses us to deny anything except the Truth of this spiritual Presence in every area of our lives. This is the central focus of all her teachings.

The first six series of Bible Interpretations were presented at her seminary in Chicago, Illinois. The remaining Series', probably close to thirty, were printed in the Inter Ocean Newspaper in Chicago. Many of the lessons are no longer available for various reasons. It is the intention of WiseWoman Press to publish as many of these Bible Interpretations as possible. Our hope is that any missing lessons will be found or directed to us.

I am very honored to join the long line of people that have been involved in publishing Emma Curtis Hopkins's Bible Interpretations. Some confusion exists as to the numbering sequence of the lessons. In the early 1920's many of the lessons were published by the Highwatch Fellowship. Inadvertently the first two lessons were omitted from the numbering system. Rev. Joanna Rogers has corrected this mistake by finding the first two lessons and restoring them to their rightful place in the order. Rev. Rogers has been able to find many of the missing lessons at the International New Thought Alliance archives in Mesa, Arizona. Rev. Rogers painstakingly scoured the archives for the missing lessons as well as for Mrs. Hopkins other works. She has published much of what was discovered. WiseWoman Press is now publishing the correctly numbered series of the Bible Interpretations.

In the early 1940's, there was a resurgence of interest in Emma's works. , At that time, Highwatch Fellowship began to publish many of her writings, and it was then that *High Mysticism*, her seminal work was published. Previously, the material contained in High Mysticism was only available as individual lessons and was brought together in book form for the first time. Although there were many errors in these first publications and many Bible verses were incorrectly quoted, I am happy to announce that WiseWoman Press is now publishing *High Mysticism* in the a corrected format. This corrected form was scanned faithfully from the original, individual lessons.

The next person to publish some of the Bible Lessons was Rev. Marge Flotron from the Ministry of Truth International in Chicago, Illinois. She published the Bible Lessons as well as many of Emma's other works. By her initiative, Emma's writings were brought to a larger audience when DeVorss & Company, a longtime publisher of Truth Teachings, took on the publication of her key works.

In addition, Dr. Carmelita Trowbridge, founding minister of The Sanctuary of Truth in Alhambra, California, inspired her assistant minister, Rev. Shirley Lawrence, to publish many of Emma's works, including the first three series of Bible Interpretations. Rev. Lawrence created mail order courses for many of these Series. She has graciously passed on any information she had, in order to assure that these works continue to inspire individuals and groups who are called to further study of the teachings of Mrs. Hopkins.

Finally, a very special acknowledgement goes to Rev Natalie Jean, who has worked diligently to retrieve several of Emma's lessons from the Library of Congress, as well as libraries in Chicago. Rev. Jean hand-typed many of the lessons she found on microfilm. Much of what she found is on her website, www.highwatch.net.

It is with a grateful heart that I am able to pass on these wonderful teachings. I have been studying dear Emma's works for fifteen years. I was introduced to her writings by my mentor and teacher, Rev. Marcia Sutton. I have been overjoyed with the results of delving deeply into these Truth Teachings.

In 2004, I wrote a Sacred Covenant entitled "Resurrecting Emma," and created a website, www.emmacurtishopkins.com. The result of creating this covenant and website has brought many of Emma's works into my hands and has deepened my faith in God. As a result of my love for these works, I was led to become a member of Wise-Woman Press and to publish these wonderful teachings. God is Good.

My understanding of Truth from these divinely inspired teachings keeps bringing great Joy, Freedom, and Peace to my life.

Dear reader; It is with an open heart that I offer these works to you, and I know they will touch you as they have touched me. Together we are living in the Truth that God is truly present, and living for and through each of us.

The greatest Truth Emma presented to us is "My Good is my God, Omnipresent, Omnipotent and Omniscient."


Rev. Michael Terranova
WiseWoman Press
Vancouver, Washington, 2010

# Lesson I

# A GOLDEN PROMISE

*Isaiah 11:1-10*

*"And there shall come forth a rod out of the stem of Jesse, and a branch shall grow out of his roots."*

Isaiah, a Hebrew prophet, writing about the time of the founding of Rome (753 B.C.), is here foretelling the coming to the world some time in the future from his own period, of a man who should know all things without instruction from any other man and do all things without any example to incite him.

There are two ways of prophesying coming events. One is by scientific information reckoned from unvarying data according to unvarying law, and the other is from the spirit of revelation when the mind opens a closed gate and discloses scenes and events about to take place or already transpired.

The prophet of revelation saw the darkness of the day on which Jesus was crucified ages before "there was darkness from the sixth unto the ninth hour."

The Chaldean astronomer calculated the eclipse of the sun for the exact date, and the astronomer at Greenwich today will agree with him that on the hills of Galilee and over the doomed walls of Jerusalem's proud temples the sun was forbidden to shine on the day of the crucifixion.

The Revelator always sees the mental or metaphysical cause for the transaction while the scientist is regulating his telescope and figuring *solis stationed* (stationary sun). History notes both with impartial pen pictures.

In Isaiah we find prophecies of a Messiah to come. When He should have come people would be different. In astronomy we read of new planetary relations necessarily affecting physical nature.

Jewish revelators were not the only ones who were expecting a great Master and Teacher and Savior to come. Egypt and India were looking for one who should understand the mystery of life and handle death and misery with the fingers of an artist skillfully transforming smeary pigments into living landscapes.

The question of ages had been then as now, "Who am I, whither am I bound and what is my mission?"

The highest philosophy of India had concluded that to "get rid of life, to get rid of living," was the only way to mastery over human conditions — unless one should come to teach them better. They said, "The passions are evil. The passions are masters of mankind, not mankind of the passions. Thus evil is master. To live knowing that old age, disease, decrepitude, death, await us, is not life that is worthwhile. Let us get rid of life — rid of the necessity for living."

So they stilled their sensations by their will and buried themselves in the sand, or lay like logs under the sal trees till the birds of the air nested on their faces and taught their young to fly from their still foreheads. Yet it availed them nothing.

The Egyptians had concluded that the "I Am" of the universe is as present in man as the gods, but only the dead must have the book telling man that he is *"I AM THAT I AM,"* for the truth at its highest is dangerous for the masses; only He that should come could live knowing truth and how to save from the evils of nature.

"Why do I feel powerful, yet the signs of my power are wanting?" they cried.

"Why should the earthquake, the tidal wave, hunger, separation, injustice, triumph of wrong over right, foil me?"

They had no answer.

They cut their flesh and went naked, cold, hungry, despised and rejected, hoping to propitiate

Deity, win worthiness of mastery — yet still no satisfaction.

They had a strange habit of blindfolding themselves and turning around and around to shut off their knowledge of where they might be, and while all their comrades waited eagerly questioning for the right way to mastery over nature, the blindfolded gave answers.

It is blessed to know that they got truth after truth in their eager searching, but mastery should be given only to him who should live the life knowing the law, obedient to law, transcending the law.

The constant mention of the true God had given the Jews of old a truer conception of Deity than any other people of the earth held, and this germ of truth should never die from among them, their prophets declared, for even in the last days of the world ten men should be found "laying hold of the skirts of him that is a Jew," saying, "We will go with you, for we have heard that you have the true God." Out of the twelve tribes of Israel there was only one left as a kingdom in Isaiah's time. That was Judah, and she was fast approaching the most ignominious humiliation. She was about to be known no more as a kingdom, but only as an outcast memory of greatness.

The twelve tribes of Israel signify the twelve divisions of the mind. They all have some spiritual word or feeling, but the tribes Israel and Judah, hold out the longest when the pressure of the material claims is great. Ten parts of the mind are easily led captive to Babylon, or the claim that "we shall all die when our time comes, suffer old age, poverty, sorrow, and none can stay us," if nature so orders.

This is not true, and two parts of the mind resent it — Israel, the spiritual feeling, and Judah, the spiritual word; but Israel the feeling, and Judah the word are not united and the feeling is lost or hidden while the word keeps on speaking.

*"The kingdom of Judah shall go down,"* said Isaiah. The martial greatness of David is a long past memory, the gorgeous victories of Solomon are ages departed. The follies of David and the adulteries of Solomon have 'wiped out the chances for worldly honors for the religious kingdom for evermore, and not until the religion of truth shall be based to its lowest point with no sign of any possibility of rising, shall the simple father of kings, Jesse, the Bethlemite, send forth from the humiliated stem or stock of his descendents, Jesus.

Isaiah knows that where the true God is named there will be always a possibility of beginning anew, like the oaks of Palestine which will bud and branch at the smell of water as long as there is a stump remaining.

Assyria, the intellect, and Egypt, the senses, may be cut down like the fir and the pine and the cedar never to flourish against spirit anymore, but though the word of truth be hushed up and shamed down, like the oak trees of Bushan, up it will spring when a Mary of Bethlehem is dedicated to Jehovah.

More than seven hundred years after Isaiah promised this rod from the stem of Jesse, Jesus came fulfilling all the prophecies. "The spirit of the Lord (the law), the spirit of wisdom, of understanding, the spirit of counsel, of might, the spirit of knowledge and of the fear of the Lord," did indeed rest upon Him.

These seven "spirits" or seven words of affirmation found by scientific reasoning were all with Him from the beginning and He needed not to be taught of them.

Isaiah makes three movements of this prophecy. First, the description of the man; second His teachings; and thirdly, the effect of His teachings when at the last the ensign or banner of God should be raised and unto it as a doctrine flashing from west to east, the gentiles or whole world should come, and "its rest should be glorious," for "they shall not hurt nor destroy in all My holy mountain."

He should know how to raise the dead, heal the sick, cast out sins, give good everywhere by His word.

The very wisest who had lived before Moses and Abraham had found out that there is a vital spark glowing within every living creature.

While this vital spark is burning through the system, life and health shine as an alabaster vase might shine with an oriental candle flaming within it. When the system gets covered with the dust of earthiness or the ways of the flesh, intellect, the vital spark, does not illuminate it, and the body wraps itself around with death.

They said, those magi of old, that the vital spark of life was not in any human being's power to restore when once it ceased to burn.

They noticed that a man might keep his physical body healthy and alive by eating and drinking and by satisfactory honors and ample possessions, up to a certain point, but beyond that point, unless he knew how to feed the vital spark so that it would spring anew within him, his end had surely come, and none could restore him.

They did not know what would rekindle or feed the vital spark of heavenly flame. They saw that though you might eat the finest flesh and drink the choicest wines, though you might have the loveliest home, and princes and potentates might flatter and fawn at your feet, this vital spark would turn away unfed, and would not glow to fan your body into life or health unless it had been fed with its own kind of food. And nobody knew what its food should be.

Jesus, who could rekindle the vital spark in the most dead of all appearances, said, *"The flesh profiteth nothing; the words that I speak unto you, they are spirit and they are life."*

He knew that the master in Israel had no rekindling quality unless he knew His words. For the vital spark which has power to keep us alive and well forevermore, will only feed on words; and, moreover, will only glow and flame when the words of Jesus are spoken. Hence there is no life outside of Christ Jesus. *"My words are life to them that find them and health to all their flesh."*

There is a science of the Christ or an orderly and systematic finding of the vital spark so that it shall glow and shine brighter and brighter, as there is a science of the stars and their movements. This science was prophesied by Isaiah as to be perfectly demonstrated by the Man who should be born in Bethlehem from the humbled stem of Jesse.

Isaiah felt as a revelator what we now know as a science, that a mind that has a word of the Christ quality whether as courage or judgment or knowledge of law, will spring forth at the least sign of hope as the stumps of the Palestine oaks will branch at the smell of water.

The coral animals that build the islands can only live in the aerated foam formed by breasting the angry billows. So some natures will only rise to breach spiritual food and demonstrate spiritual vitality when the heavy waters of sorrow, defeat, ignominy, beat them back.

King Bruce of Scotland felt his noble courage faltering when pursued by enemies and distrusted by friends. At the sight of a persevering little spider defeated again and again in its attempt to rise to a certain height on its tiny thread, but finally at the tenth effort succeeding, Bruce sprang to his feet. "Shall a Bruce have less courage than a spider?" he cried, and he put forth the rod of his courage to victory.

"Build on resolve and not upon regret."

Whoever faces the deepest feeling that stirs him when failure seems to have him down will find that there is a conviction within his own soul that he has a right to success. This is the vital spark ready to flame if you feed it with words.

"Thy word was a lamp unto my feet and a light (or guide) unto my path." The hunger of this fire of the soul can only be fed by the strongest words you have ever heard.

In the science we learn to face all the feelings with right words till the whole body glows and the whole character flames with good health, good judgment, and hospitality along every line.

Now the world has the words that will fan the vital spark through all the being into a health out of the reach of sickness, a peace out of the reach of pain, a life out of the reach of death, a success out of the reach of defeat. The world must not deny this. The world must not listen when the most popular magazine of the day tells us that all mankind now rests under the era of bafflement and despair. It must not believe the scholars when they tell that only those plays and songs and preachers describing defeated man are popular. The world must not believe anybody who says that the Omar Khayam pictures of the soul flying desolate are more popular than the songs of deliverance and the teachers of triumph.

When the actor impersonating the potter struggling to revive the lost art of the Tatswood pottery is at the last day likely to fail because no one will even give him a hod of coal, yet the fires of his ever-young soul springs up crying, "I will begin again!" And if then you fail. "Begin again!" Why does the audience, away to the galleries, applaud if to be defeated absolutely is more popular than to rise on the wings of the words of the soul? "Success and not failure is my birthright."

Isaiah understands how to teach a nation, a religious body, a man, what is true, better than the teachers of today, for he sees the Man whom we, 2500 years after him, call Messiah, smite the whole earth with the words of His twelve lessons of life science, and that the profoundest doctrine ever enunciated is, "Judge not after the sight of the eyes, nor after the hearing of the ears," for so shall thy Master teach thee, Himself fulfilling the law. When ye shall "judge not according to appearance" they shall not hurt nor destroy in all My holy mountain.

The prophecy reads that they that shut their eyes and stop their ears from evil shall dwell on high. Their bread shall be sure. Their waters shall not fail. They shall partake of the living substance, even the word of God.

"There is a substance pervading all the worlds of the universe," said the philosophers of antiquity. It fills all things. It is too fine for the senses to recognize. It is only handled by the words of the mind. Nay, the words of the mind are too coarse to handle this substance that pervades all things; it must be touched only by the understanding of the mind. And the understanding of truth is the only touch fine enough to mold this substance, which is Truth itself.

Out of it is made happiness, peace, delight. This substance is Truth, Truth is God. God is the only substance. Only they who know that it is not truth which call us bones and flesh and nerves; only they who know that it is not truth which says that there are any thoughts or any substance out of which to make evil, can touch the mount where there is nothing to hurt or destroy.

How fine is the writing on the "ensign" Isaiah saw should be lifted up in these days!

Is not this the acme of "judging not according to the sight of the eyes nor the hearing of the ears," when we know that it as bad for the preacher of the wickedness of killing as it is for the slayer to slay, for:

*"He who thinks that he can slay a life —*

*Or he who thinks life can be slain —*

*These both do err, for life is God,*

*And God cannot be slain."*

There is no substance out of which to make one who can kill. There is no substance out of which to make one who thinks such things can happen.

There is only God.

Isaiah says that the gentiles will hasten to rest under this banner.

"And its rest shall be glorious!"

Ho! Ye who toil and labor to earn your bread; rest under this teaching. Your rest shall be on the topless mount of the living God, Christ Jesus has come.

Rest, pale mother, under the ensign of the truth Jesus Christ taught — there is only God — and the reviving winds of the hilltops of Paradise shall fan your white brow and set your tired feet among the green fields of love, and your "rest shall be glorious."

Come, world-weary traveler, drink from this water of the life Christ Jesus preached — listen not to the noise of the teachers of bafflement and despair — the triumphant song of your own soul defies them. Captivity is led captive. Christ Jesus has come, and they that come under His ensign know no evil. For them God the good is all.

*January 3, 1892*

# Lesson II

# THE TWELVE GATES

*Isaiah 26:1-10*

Here is a lesson in prophecy. Isaiah sees ahead from his own time into a period never yet reached (externally) when all the nations will speak truth. And with their speaking truth there should be salvation in the very stones of the walls of the city.

All the time Isaiah is writing you will notice that he believes intensely in time. He foretells the good future of the race. He sees the golden age to come.

Such men as Isaiah have had a great deal to do with the civilized world's looking forward to the coming of God as Father, Son and Holy Spirit, instead of knowing and realizing that God, as the Giver of every good and satisfactory condition, is always here in His greatest power and greatest beneficence, ready to pour out into visible gifts what lies so closely around us.

Any strong mind with intense conviction can set the current of the world's thought flowing when it speaks.

So Isaiah set the current of the world's thought consciously where his words were read, and unconsciously where they were only felt, into the belief in a far-off future for its good. The very best kind of men the race has had, with only one or two marked exceptions, have believed in future good instead of insisting upon all things now.

Your bodily health should be perfect now, whether Isaiah believed you should wait for a golden age for it or not. Your mind should be perfect in its judgment so that you should speak no error and make no mistake now, Isaiah and all the rest of the prophets to the contrary notwithstanding. Your prosperity along every line of effort should be delightfully satisfactory every minute now. All the prophets of Israel and the preachers of the ages should be rejected if they speak contrariwise.

Jesus Christ says, *"Now is the day of salvation."* He is not pleased that John the Baptist is always telling of what is to come. He says that the very least spiritually-minded to be in the kingdom — not going into it — is greater. The kingdom of health — health is God — is here waiting our seeing and loving it. The kingdom of judgment — judgment is God — is here waiting our seeing and loving it. The kingdom of prosperity — prosperity is God — is here waiting our seeing and loving it. One is no more material than another.

In the old high Jewish science of God prosperity was always a sign of God's recognized presence. There must be also good health and noble judgment to accompany prosperity, else we will be one-sided.

If you are afraid to lay hold on prosperity as a marked sign of favor from the Most High, you show that some great error of a man or set of men struggling to be spiritually-minded has got hold of your thoughts to push them his or their way.

Jesus Christ owned all the kingdoms of this world and the riches of them. "Know ye not that Jesus Christ is in you?"

Take special notice that Jesus Christ assures you and all the race that being spiritually-minded you are sure to have a hundredfold more in this sphere of experience and in the realm of high thoughts where you go. By continually keeping His name you have everlasting rest in delightful companionship, unbroken family life, abundant blessings greater than you can ask or even think.

The kingdom of God is an everlasting kingdom lying around us. To speak of it as here and now is to open our eyes to see it. Many a man has grown old still hoping to be prospered when he might have taken the prosperity held out to him from the first by saying, "I am prosperous now and I am awake to see it. I do not believe in waiting to get what is my right today."

It is about time the world got out from under the swing of people's thoughts of futures. The Buddhists teach, and so did the Egyptians long ago, that we ought to cry "IT IS! IT IS!" to the good.

A good physician is one who believes that his powders and pills will work now. If he hands his successful pills and powders to a man who believes that maybe sometime he will be a successful doctor, those pills and powders won't work through the future kind of mind unless that mind yields absolutely to the now feeling of the successful one.

You can take the successful note of now from your own reason, or you can get near some successful man or woman and get a treatment from their confident mental quality.

I do not believe in poor Christians. I have seen people get quite well of their crooked limbs who lost all their means after being quite subservient in mind to one who thought healed legs were a sign of spiritual life, but who felt that prosperity was not a sign of spiritual life.

Elisha, who lived about 100 years before Isaiah, did not speak so powerfully as Isaiah; if he had we would be much more prosperous now than we seem to be.

Elisha picked up dead people and said, "Live now!" He fed hundreds of people out of small provisions right when they were hungry. He saw how mean it would be to promise pottage to starving people in a golden age to come.

Once when he was living in the little village of Dothan the Syrian king sent a host of soldiers to slay him. Elisha's servant was terrified, but Elisha calmly said, "They that be with us are more than they that be with them." And looking around about towards the hills of Samaria the servant saw chariots and horses and majestic horsemen fighting their cause, and there was no army of Syrians could hurt Elisha. Do you believe this? It would be a good plan for you to believe that if you think what is true with all your might that all the supernal beings of the world of God are on your side.

Do not wait for danger and privation to swoop down on you like a wind from the strong errors of the prophets and priests and ministers of the past in conjunction with the present overpowering belief in the reality and law of such things. Rise and think for yourself and then when the day of calamity seems to be about to destroy you, you will find the thoughts you now take up will encamp in the hills around about you and put all evils to flight.

I suppose you understand that those majestic horseman and chariots of fire were the outpicturing of Elisha's affirmations.

"Have your feet shod with the preparation of the gospel." Today think the bravest and noblest and richest thoughts you can speak. Think them well. They will come back as good health, good judgment, prosperity. "He createth the fruit of the lips."

Words come back in fruits of all kinds. Just hear the beggars scream. Who made them beggars? Isaiah, John the Baptist, the pulpits of modern times and all such as agree that good health, good judgment, and prosperity are going to belong to mankind in the future.

*"Now is the day of salvation,"* says Jesus.

*"Open ye the gates,"* said Isaiah. He meant open your mind to speak boldly the twelve words of science.

The twelve gates of revelation and prophecy and science are the twelve knowledges you already possess. The moment you hear from the roar of without, the words that are not true, you begin to close your gates. Open the twelve gates boldly. Swing open the gates of that wonderful wisdom given you from the foundation of the world. Regard nobody's teaching who believes in the power of evil. Avoid books that describe evil. Ignore people who believe in evil. Open wide the twelve gates of your noble city and shed abroad the glory of health, strength, joy, prosperity.

Do you know the twelve laws that are shut up within your wonderful mind? You had better hear them spoken boldly by somebody who knows them and believes in them, but I will give them briefly for you to speak either silently or audibly.

Remember that what you think is a wave of light going through the mental atmosphere of the world, and wherever your true thought strikes, somebody will be lifted off a bed of pain or healed of some sorrow.

*******

1. There is good for me. My God is my good, my life, my truth, my love, my substance, my intelligence, omnipresent, omnipotent, omniscient.

2. There is no mixture of evil in my good. There is no opposition to my God as material conditions of any kind. There is no absence of life, substance, intelligence. There is nothing to hate. There is no presence of sin, sickness, or death in my world, where God is the only presence and power and wisdom.

3. God is all. God is the omnipresent, omnipotent, omniscient good, as life, truth, love, substance, intelligence. I am my own idea of God, and I live and move and have my being according to my idea of God. I am spirit, mind, like my God, and shed abroad wisdom, strength, holiness. My God works through me to will and to do that which ought to be done by me. I am governed by the true God and am kept from sin, from suffering for sin, and I cannot fear sin, sickness or death.

4. I do believe that the true God is now working with me and through me and by me and for me, to make me a living demonstration of omnipresent, omnipotent, omniscient goodness.

5. As spirit, I can preach the gospel, heal the sick, cast out demons, raise the dead.

6. I understand the secret of instantaneous spiritual demonstration.

7. I hold no accusations against the people of God. I do not believe in lustful passions or sensual appetites. I believe that all these are the hunger and thirst after righteousness, given a false name.

8. I do not accuse the people of God of deceiving each other or of being deceived. There is no opposition to truth.

9. I do not accuse the people of God of being sinners. It is true that all things were made by the true God and are now very good.

10. I do not believe in a mixture of good and evil in the universe. I stand to my confidence that all is good. All is good in truth. According to my faith so it is now unto me and unto those about me.

11. I cannot admit that there is any foolishness or ignorance or weakness or old age failure in omnipresent, omnipotent, omniscience. There is but one mind, and that is God — one substance and that is God.

12. The white soul of every creature stands out ransomed from sin, death and sorrow by the words of truth. The whole world is awake to righteousness. Time is no more. All is well now.

Judging not after the sight of the eyes nor after the hearing of the ears, these twelve gates will open and you will surely see things as they are and not as has been believed they are.

To live and think these thoughts is to shine as the sun with love and wisdom.

This was the truth as lived by Jesus Christ. This is the truth Jesus Christ lives. This is the truth everlasting.

High over all principalities and powers of unbelief in the allness of God, high over all memories of your past, high out of reach of your fears of the future, live and reign in truth with Jesus Christ in you and with you and by you and for you.

Do you not know that this truth is Jesus Christ in you? Do you not know that when you speak this truth it is Jesus Christ opening the gates of glory for your world?

Poor Isaiah looked forward to a time when the world should know it. We rise in the triumph of knowing that the kingdom of God is within us all now.

*January 10, 1892*

# Lesson III

# WHO ARE DRUNKARDS

*Isaiah 28:1-13*

The lesson for today is all about woe, according to Isaiah and the religious world that has let its thought currents be stirred by Isaiah. It is, *"Woe to the crown of pride, to the drunkards of Ephraim;"* and the Golden text selected is, *"Wine is a mocker, strong drink is raging, and whosoever is deceived thereby is not wise."*

According to absolute truth, who are drunkards? Those who have swallowed the idea that there is another power besides spirit, another substance besides spirit, another law besides spirit.

What other power besides spirit is there? None. "Is there any besides Me? Nay, I know not any."

What other substance is there besides spirit? None. "Do not I fill heaven and earth?"

What other law is there besides the law of the spirit? None. "The law of the spirit maketh free from sin and death." *"There shall be one Lord (law) and His name one."*

Then who is there to swallow the idea that there is more than one power, presence, law? Nobody.

There is but one being. "There is one God who is above you all and through you all and in you all."

Then who is there to be a drunkard? Nobody.

Then what is Isaiah talking about in this twenty-eighth chapter? Nothing.

How, then is it profitable to read and study the chapter? Simply as the observation of contrasts — opposites. To look his words over from the standpoint of one who knows what is real and what is supposition is worthwhile.

If there were anybody to believe in two powers and the results of the belief were to confront us this would be the way the results would look. But starting out with the belief in evil and good would not make both evil and good true, any more than it would make it true if you should suspect a good man of having stolen your watch when he was utterly incapable of such a thing.

God is the only Presence, Power, Law. You may agree with Isaiah and the kings and queens and college presidents of the world that drunkenness and poverty and sorrow are realities and are permitted within the omnipresent good, but it is a lie from the beginning just the same and you will only demonstrate freedom in yourself and for your world by rising out of the clutches of Isaiah and the kings and queens and college presidents by speaking the truth.

*"You shall know the truth and the truth shall set you free."*

If there were any being to get drunk then he must have first swallowed the belief in two powers, two substances, two laws. Then he would get afraid of the other power and get to hating the other presence. Then his hate must rest somewhere and on something as the magnetic belts that are supposed to circle the earth find some stones, some plants, some animals that will catch and hold their quality of magnetism more than others.

If a person keeps saying, even casually and carelessly, "I hate it," or "I hate him," his words must go over the airs like dandelion seeds and drop somewhere, and whoever comes into the spots where the words are lying will pick up the harmless little nightshade or tobacco plant and find poison in it. He will find the word hate dropped into the plant and will say it is poison.

But it would never be true for a moment. For *"God saw everything that He had made and, behold, it was very good." "And without Him was nothing made that was made."* Ephraim in this woe of Isaiah is Samaria which was named after Ephraim. Ephraim means double fruitfulness — that is, both evil and good thoughts should have their fruits in this city. They should have their crown here. They should be very apparent.

Isaiah falls directly into the sight of both good and evil, and one moment triumphantly prophesies the double good to be demonstrated when people shall not judge after the sight of the eyes, and in the next moment judges entirely after the sight of his eyes by seeing where the hate thoughts of Esau had stopped in the vineyards and among the people of Samaria. Ephraim or Samaria took the hate thoughts of Esau and the fear thoughts of Jacob, and Isaiah saw the feeling effects of such notions so vividly that he caused the hate and fear to come quickly to a head, like a great boil, and break over in to a terrible rage of misery. For Isaiah believed greatly in the active operation of evil now and the future active operation of good.

His mind had great power. At Samaria he might have pronounced the omnipotence of the good with such intense spiritual and mental efficiency that the reeling priests and drunken princes would have shouted praises and hallelujahs to Jehovah Nissi ( Jehovah is my banner).

The banner over them was love. The belief around them was hate. Where did all the hate come from? It had slipped over the head of Ephraim himself from Esau's hatred of Jacob, had rested temporarily on poor Joseph, sold by his brethren in to Egypt, and had come down to reach its ultimate or crown of pride in Samaria.

Isaiah ought to have realized how powerful — how doubly powerful the word of good would be in Samaria, just as Elisha had so long before him.

Just at the moment when the hate thoughts of Esau and the fear thought of Jacob were festered into what was called the siege of Samaria, Elisha had risen in the power of his mind and spoken such words as had turned the Syrian army aside, and fed the starving inhabitants of the city where forever the signs of evil and of good together should distract the mind to see double, as the Iceland spar doubly refracts light, and forever makes two images of one substance — till we withdraw our hate thoughts from the earth.

Whoever sees both good and evil plays the part of a double refractor, and is typified by the Iceland spar. He is well represented by Isaiah if he feels dreadfully about the evil and works himself sick in the slums, supposing that to mourn and wail and pronounce woes on governments, preachers, teachers, for not stopping the same is wise. Such ragings are deceptions, and "whoever is deceived thereby is not wise."

Back of all that the senses tell, and back of all that the mind believes, is the truth. Whoever started there, and believed in something not true, he caused a Jacob to be both mean and noble. There are two Jacobs now. Jacob stole his birthright and earned Rachel. These two trains of character fought within him near the brook of Jabbok. He was trying to believe in the triumph of love while his mind was half believing in the power of hate.

The confidence in the power and presence and efficiency or law of love is never absent from anybody's mind; but not everybody rallies that idea (which is his angel), and causes it to face the fear of hate, or fear of evil, as Jacob did just before he met Esau.

His confidence in the power of love prevailed, and love spoke boldly as his noble friend, "As a prince hast thou power with God and man."

Take your two states of mind and settle the question today whether you believe in the presence and power and working of the love of God to stop all the fruits of hate and fear now. See how Jacob prevailed. Esau met him kindly. Your mission is greater than Jacob's. He settled it for himself, but not for his children nor for his world. You and I will take the question for all the universe.

I do believe in the good only as now working with me and through me and by me and for me to make me a living demonstration of the power of goodness for all the world. I do not believe in the signs of evil. God is all. God folds and keeps all this world in love. I pronounce all evil sights and sounds absent, and declare love and joy their rightful inheritance of every creature, from this moment.

If the absurdity of such a prayer comes up it is your Jacob experience. Rise and wrestle to believe in the good. Miracles are wrought by prayer, child of God.

When fear of evil or hate of evil sights or belief in a law of evil comes up within you, wrestle; wrestle all night till the morning. You will see great corporations wither and drunken officials cease from power and proud magnates get meek as Jacob's thigh — which was the part of him that stood for his fear of evil — as these are the part of the world that stand out as your fear of evil or grief at evil.

Jacob was most interested in his own fortunes. You are interested in a common humanity. What you have you wish all the world to have. They may receive it at your hands. If you believe otherwise than this, wrestle with my message for it is sent to tell you that our God reigns and you will see His loving kindness when you believe He is the only presence, the only power, and the only efficiency.

At Samaria, Elisha decided for the loving kindness of Jehovah. At Samaria, Jesus announced the presence of the Messiah. At Samaria, Isaiah pronounced for the power of evil as ending in death.

The noble vineyards, the beautiful olive groves, and the bountiful fields of waving grain in Samaria were the fruit of the word of the loving kindness of God believed in. The intoxicating wines, the reeling priests, and profligate princes were the fruits of the words of hate and the belief in hate.

As there is only one presence and that is omnipresent, only one power and that is omnipotence, only one science or knowledge and that is omniscience, any other idea of anything must be no idea at all — just delusion.

Whenever one has tried the ways of the world and learned the law of the spirit there comes a time when he must choose positively which he will believe in. It will mark itself on his face from that moment, for he has met his Samaria, and the watch-post thereof is in him from that time on. Samaria means "watch-post."

The woman at the well still under the dominion of the Isaiah type of a future Messiah heard Jesus Christ tell her that the Messiah was already here. We who have been believing that the good is coming to us now rise to shake off the belief in time and the belief in the presence of evil and declare that there is nothing to hate. We declare from the coiling cobra to the flowing bowl of the reeling statesmen we withdraw our accusations.

There is nothing to hate. God made all things and pronounced them very good. We will not fill them with our fear of them. We know that this is the only law of safety there is. It is the law of non-condemnation practiced by Jesus Christ, *"Neither do I condemn thee."* So shall it be fulfilled of which He promised, *"They shall drink any deadly thing and it shall not hurt them."*

We will remember how God made everything good, even all mankind, and will not accuse anybody of anything. There we will see our high thoughts come around us instead of our low thoughts. The high thoughts of Abraham came and sat in the door of his tent like men. The high thoughts of Elijah took him up in a chariot of majesty. The high thoughts of Elisha encamped as Majestic horsemen and descended the walls of Samaria to tell him how to feed the besieged city. The high thoughts of Jesus fed Him, as an angel came and ministered. All the people round about us are majestic, noble, beautiful, happy.

If we have covered them with mantles of meanness, with veils of dishonesty, with skins of ugliness, with talks of misery, we hereby withdraw all the thoughts which have caused them to look and act quite different from their true selves, and we know that so shall the supernal beings God keeps in this world — the angels of whom we are unaware — come into our sight. All is good. All is beauty. All is love. Here, on the hilltop of Samaria, we lift our eyes to God and pronounce no woe on mankind, no denunciation on the creeping things, nor on the growing plants or fruit.

There is no process by which any man can hurt his neighbor according to spirit. And spirit is all. There is no way whereby man can defraud his neighbor according to spirit. And spirit is all. There is no law whereby anything that lives or grows can cause our young men to reel or stagger as drunken. There is only God. There are no words given under Heaven for anybody to eat save the words of Jesus Christ. *"They shall have no power to hurt."*

Do you not see that if you must rise today and announce to your own self whether you accuse anything or anybody, or withdraw your accusation, that there is but one thing to do?

If you have noticed how no other plan works you may be more willing to withdraw your accusations for a new plan. Whosoever is deceived by thinking that it is wine that causes men to reel had better withdraw his accusation from the wine and see it "have no power to hurt." Whosoever thinks that strong drink is raging as a wild enemy to peace and prosperity had better withdraw his fear of evil and his belief in hate and his sting of accusation from the air where they have wondered and dropped into the fermented grains, and strong drink shall have no power to hurt even when mixed with the deadly drugs that represent our hatred of people.

"They shall drink any deadly thing and it shall not hurt them."

The stings of our false notions we now withdraw. We love truth and good substance. "If this be not true then is my preaching vain," and I must enter the gates of despair with the rest of the philanthropists of the world who believe in fighting the evils their own beliefs have projected on the canvas of humanity.

But I do not believe in the power or the presence or the action of evil. At the highest point of its crown of pride I name it delusion and put there the triumphant healing name — Jesus Christ.

*"There is, therefore, now no condemnation."*

There is nothing to hate. All is spirit. This is the teaching prophesied to come; "Hear and your soul shall live."

*"We feel the air blow o'er us.*

*And the glory shines before us*

*Of what mankind may be.*

*Pure, generous, brave and free."*

"Am I my brother's keeper?" Yea, verily.

But the beasts of the field were made to love me, the storms were made to praise me, and I was made to love them all   There is nothing to hate.

*January 17, 1892*

# Lesson IV

# AWAKE THOU THAT SLEEPEST

*Isaiah 37:1-21*

Here is a lesson that tells religious people — truly God-loving people — what to do today with the great trust combinations, the soulless corporations and unequal opportunities of human beings on the planet.

Now, the naming of these things does not make them realities by any means, any more than naming and describing a nightmare makes it a reality, though all its Gorgons have seemed more real than the presence of your loving mother near you all the time.

We name what seems evil in order to take away its appearance, or seeming.

It is a great nightmare which insists that in a world occupied by the good entirely, any other actions can be going on except good. Then the whole business of those who know that it is only a dream is to awaken the world to truth. Paul cried, *"Awake, thou that sleepest!"*

The object lesson which is here presented from Isaiah Chapter 37, is the explicit direction to us, and by following it we can stop this great amassing of riches at the expense of the helpless (so described) and the strange situation of a few able to withhold opportunities from the many.

Historically the object lesson was placed on the boards 712 B.C. Hezekiah was a good and pious King of Judah. Sennacherib was the idolatrous King of the powerful Assyrians. They met in battle in exactly the same way we will meet in battle the Assyrian monarch, capitalization of today.

Hezekiah set his idea of God out plainly before all the people in the temple. You will notice that he never compromised his description of God by admitting for an instant that it was God who permitted the Assyrians to get such powerful odds against Jerusalem.

In the science of mind it is very important that we speak accurately, just as it is very important that we say four and two are six in a great problem in trigonometry. Mind builds all conditions and circumstances. Then, of course, we must have truth in the mind to build true conditions and circumstances.

If Hezekiah had said once that it was their duty to be "resigned to the troubles God had in His providence assigned to them," the silent victory here recorded could never have taken place.

It is no credit to our reason to be setting up a straw or stone Gorgon to knock down; so it is no credit to our judgment to be setting up such errors in our minds as that God in His providence has seen fit to do this or that which has hurt so sorely.

Only by the accurate description of their God could Hezekiah have defeated with his little handful of material power the army of 185,000 Assyrians pitted against Jerusalem.

Only by the accurate description of God can we defeat the solid phalanx of material riches pitted against the just rights of mankind today. Fighting the princes and magnates of the planet will not make them less. It will only put the power from them into the hands of ruffians, who will not be half as wise in dealing with it as those already in power are.

Hezekiah, with his kingdom, had been having a long, hard struggle to live against such a state of affairs, just as the good and honest people of today feel that they have a hard time to get on in the world with such great corporations chewing them up and working against them all the time, while dishonesty seems to flourish and goodness is laughed at.

Sennacherib, the king of a great corporation that has swallowed all the smaller enterprises of the whole country round about, sent word to

Hezekiah that if he would work in his interests he would feed and clothe and house him well. He told Hezekiah it was no use for him to stand up and declare that the invisible Lord Jehovah would or could defend Jerusalem against him because so far everything had been obliged to yield. He mentioned the mining interests, the manufacturing interests, the political machinery, the shipping interests, educational efforts (under the term "gods," of course) that had already succumbed entirely and now he advises religion to do likewise.

Hezekiah never answered Sennacherib in words face to face. He took the letter that described how everything was yielding and "spread it before the Lord." Then he said, "It is true that all these interests," under the symbolic names of "kingdoms," of course, "have succumbed to Sennacherib whose god was Nisroch (Monopoly) but none of these interests of humanity have stood forth and declared themselves under the unfailing protection of the Lord God Almighty."

"No, they had all hoped to fight materiality with materiality (mentioned as material God against material God, of course). But as for me, I do not believe in meeting evil with evil, matter with matter. I do not believe that there is any need of martyrdom or suffering or failure or defeat of any kind for those who trust in the true God."

Then Hezekiah declared his highest ideal of God. Hear him. There is no "flinchy" speaking of yielding to Sennacherib's hosts, "if it be the Lord's will." He knows, if he knows anything, that his highest ideal of the Divine Being is not of one who has to do evil that good may come. If he had admitted that idea into his description of God he would have been setting up a less than the true God, and an imaginary God cannot meet Sennacherib's host. Mind that.

Today we cannot try any halfway God on the situation. This description of Hezekiah's is the only true one; *"O, Lord of Hosts, God of Israel, that dwelleth between the cherubim* (of love and protection*), Thou art the God, even Thou alone, of all the kingdoms of the earth. Thou hast made heaven and earth. Save us that all the kingdoms of the earth may know that Thou are the Lord, even Thou only."*

As he thus described his highest ideal of God, the thought went over to the camp of the Assyrians, whose soldiers were the personified beliefs in the power of trusts and monopolies, and 185,000 men lay "dead corpses" without the sound of a battering ram, or arrow, or stone.

The greatest fight of the ages was in idea. And the two ideas that fought were the perfect description of God and the imagination of what God is.

The might of the gentiles, unsmote by the sword, hath melted like snow in the glance of the Lord.

*"For the weapons of our warfare are not carnal, but mighty through God to the putting down of strongholds."*

And now, who is there to arise in the power of his might for the honor of the good, and describe his highest idea, of the good as having the right to reign? The only reason Sennacherib and his hosts have come down upon the world in spite of religious teachings, is because the highest idea, of what ought to be, has not been described as what is.

The speaking out from the silence where the ideal has always been hidden by the repetition of the nonsense that "God, in His inscrutable wisdom, permits evil, to which we must bow our heads," is the divine "glance of truth" which will lay every trust company, every unjust corporation, every unrighteous scheme, low as Sennacherib's host.

On even a small scale of human experience this principle will work. It is better for those people who have been threatened with poverty and want through any sort or kind of combination of hard luck against them, to make up their mind what their highest ideal of God is and talk to it and tell it what they expect of such a character.

Write down your highest ideal. Read it over. If you have cut under the truth of the true God you must erase that part and make it right. Only the highest idea can come against the culmination of the series of errors in the algebra of human experience wherewith no value stands for soul, all value.

No preaching but the highest ideality can meet Sennacherib's host of believers that the god Nisroch (monopoly of the goods of the world) is in rule.

The highest ideal is the only real. It has been kept silent by our not speaking it forth. We are the word. We speak as we please — that which we speak stands forth. No compromise. The true God is that "Thou Only" of Hezekiah.

The actual conscious speaking or thinking of truth has an astonishing effect upon hosts of minds. Any idea that is right will accomplish wonders of good by laying hosts of nightmares low.

For instance, a few years ago somewhere a man or woman who had believed in sickness and disease as a part of their inheritance, and had tried every material thing in creation from foreign travel to honeybees' stings and southern flies thought suddenly as all these things had failed there was nothing more to do but to do nothing. Accordingly that hitherto unsuccessful invalid determined to do nothing. The same idea went on the wings of the winds and simultaneously all over the planet chronics of a certain type of mind determined to lie still and see what would become of them.

That was a beautiful state of mind. The silence into which they committed themselves is the ideal where all good lies waiting. They all got well.

Their old maladies dropped down like Sennacherib's host. Afterwards certain of them said they thought of God as a healing presence while they lay there. It came to them that God is health and not sickness. Others said they felt that the silence is nature's restorative; *vis medicatris naturaet.* (the healing power of nature) "In the silence, God speaketh to my soul."

In great sickness or pain or trouble lie very still. Lie still as death. Down through your mind will fall the healing God.

In such cases as this, however, carefully describe your highest ideal of God and tell it what you expect of it. Don't compromise. Don't give in because you remember what good people have suffered, I tell you they need not have suffered if they had believed in the true God. Cut out of your mind such memories. Cut out of your mind that you want the will of God to be done. The will of your old trouble-sending deity isn't worth remembering.

Just read how unconditioned Great Hezekiah's God was, and, bearing in mind what great things the unconditioned God accomplished for him, insist on His doing the same for you.

There is a little side lesson in this one of Hezekiah's demonstration, which is useful as showing how lovingly there is a goodness shaping our ends for us which we may have demonstrated in the smallest items.

Hezekiah's name meant "Strength of Jehovah." Thus he had all strength on his side. He ought to have just given thanks for his strength just as Jesus Christ always did before a miracle. You will see that Hezekiah was a trifle afraid of the strength of materiality — of the opposing conditions. Without entering into any explanation of how this shows that "in our greatest strength," we cannot help seeing that each person's name stands for his easiest honors and also for his greatest errors or weaknesses. If anyone knows the significance of his own name he knows what it is he can demonstrate most quickly.

The shadow of that great good is always the fear that things are exactly the opposite. If your name is Rebekah you are chained to prosperity, and by pulling on the principle of bounty by your giving thanks that you have such great possessions belonging to you, they will come flying into your sight.

Very likely you are complaining of poverty and crying with longings the very moments when you ought to be giving thanks that your highest ideal of prosperity is yours now.

Suppose your name is William. Whatever you put after the two words "I am" will demonstrate promptly. Very likely you will have very intense experiences, because you speak well of yourself sometimes, and ill of yourself sometimes. You should identify yourself with the highest Name you know. You should be like Jesus Christ, and be so at one with truth that you cannot distinguish between truth and yourself. You remember that He said, "I am truth." The highest ideal you can conceive — you are it. You can say "I am Omnipotent Spirit" and prove it.

Suppose your name is Francis. Your birthright is freedom. You should say often "I am free." Probably you have a great habit of getting under the personal influence of other people. The instant you get under them your judgment gets biased.

Your name may be Mary, and your affirmation ought to be, "I am honored and glorified." But very likely you are given to mourning because your human experience is bitter.

This is one of the little side lessons off from the main one of the Hezekiah prayer for deliverance, but the good that folds us around, waiting to be announced, blesses even the tiniest item of our life when we acknowledge it.

*"Acknowledge Me in all thy ways* (in the smallest transactions and situations) *and I will direct thy paths."* Set your mind steadfastly to the name and the character of the good according to your ideal.

That highest good is the real. The ideal is the real. No matter how silent you have hitherto been on the subject now is the time to rise with the right description of the true God. There will be no more pain, no more poverty, no more discord in your life, with the acknowledgment that is right.

What is your name? You were not named carelessly. The word that you bear is your word that will come flying to demonstrate itself when you speak it and bravely refuse the easiest error into which you are habitually slipping.

Who is a God like the true God? Who redeemeth all life from destruction, who healeth all diseases, who crowneth with loving kindness everything and everybody, every instant, save only the true God? How great and efficient and kind is your God?

That one whom you have been describing is the one who dealt with you up to date.

*January 24, 1892*

# Lesson V

# THE HEALING LIGHT

*Isaiah 53:1-12*

*"Who hath believed our report? And to whom is the arm of the Lord revealed?"*

If we were the least bit under the spell of Isaiah's powerful mind, we would be just as majestically mournful at the apparent unbelief of this age in the teachings of Jesus Christ as Isaiah was at the age he anticipated.

But we will not be biased by Isaiah's belief in evil and the power of evil. We will take his own words that the highest possible doctrine is refusing to judge after the sight of the eyes and after the hearing of the ears. We will look straight into the meanings of the words of the Messiah Himself, when He says *"I am Truth,"* and *"According to thy faith be it unto thee;"* also, *"For the lightest word thou shalt give account."* Therefore, *"Judge not according to appearance, but judge righteous judgment."*

People often have premonitions of evil. They do not know the law of the annulling power of their own words, and so they wait until the premonitions come to pass, and tell the papers and magazines what a mysterious faculty they have for prophecy.

That premonitive instinct which they have is the signal that it is at that moment time for them to use a power they really do possess, which is that of preventing calamities. If you have a foreboding feeling, it is the sign that you ought to speak certain words.

Knowing the power of words you can speak the right ones promptly and heartily. *"Thou shalt decree a thing and it shall be established unto thee; when men are cast down then thou shalt say, there is lifting up."*

A clergyman of the recognized and dominant faith (that is in school and satan and afflictions from God) was a very beloved pastor in sickness. He had a cheerful face and fatherly manner that comforted all kinds and classes of people. He had been many years accustomed to visiting his parish sick and had learned to be quite wise in detecting symptoms and advising precautions. There was always one sign that he knew as the foreshadowing of what is called death. It never failed to herald that strange belief of mankind. When he realized an imperceptible (to the eyes) purplish haze he knew its forewarning.

After a while he heard of this law of the right word as able to destroy sickness, sin and death and once when he saw the hitherto unfailing signal he determined to speak it away if there was such a thing. So he said to the purplish haze, "Once I knew you as the sign of death, but now I do not believe in death, nor in the signs of death; I believe only in life and the signs of life. Life is God Omnipotent. I pronounce you the sign of renewing, vigorous life for this man, in the name of the Father, and of the Son and of the Holy Ghost." The purple haze lifted and the red blood tinged the cheeks and fingers of the sick man.

Isaiah saw the rejection of the Redeemer as a coming state of affairs under the law of the fruitage of error. But why did he not blast the fruits of error while they were in the leaf-time of their spring greenness, 712 years B.C., just as Jesus blasted the fig tree before the figs ripened, to illustrate the power of truth to stop error before it comes to fruitage?

Did not Isaiah know enough of the meaning of the passage, "and the Lord repented," to know that the law of the good (or the Lord) can always be spoken in time to turn back (or repent) anything not good?

It is perfectly astonishing how much power of vision Isaiah had to see both evil and good fruits, like a helpless spectator. If he had spoken vehemently that according to the law of error the world would reject Jesus Christ first and His teachings afterwards, but he pronounced error null and void and its results nothingness, his stupendous mind would have drawn the curtains of darkness to the right and the left from the age when Jesus came, and they would have seen Him in His true light. Then again, Isaiah ought to have told our age that we should see the reasonableness of the ideal and would not reject it when it should come announced as plain judgment of goodness.

It seems verily as if we had no mind so manifestly powerful as Isaiah's now, because nobody has seemed to rouse out of the belief in future as strongly as Isaiah rose out of his age when destruction lay upon it and announced coming prosperity.

*"To whom is the arm of the Lord revealed?"* That is, who sees this law not that Jesus Christ has taught it, so plainly that he can demonstrate the power thereof? Arms are symbols of power in the scriptures. Who sees plainly the power of the good over all evil, even to the annihilation thereof, present, as Isaiah saw the future demonstration of the good? So this lesson teaches us over again the necessity of declaring that the truth about things is now just as much as it ever was or ever will be. Heaven is now and here. It never will be any more here than it is now. But who says this strongly? So Isaiah mourns because he saw us speaking in our dream of error very feebly like people asleep and muttering.

There used to be a theory that this world is all asleep. While we are lying still on our beds in dreamless sleep we are in the normal and natural condition, as we noticed that the sickest, most pained or troubled creature is well enough if he is asleep in dreamless peace. That all what we call waking is not true waking, but nightmare — pure nightmare. That all this time we are at home in our "Father's house where the many mansions be," and only need to speak the right word in this our nightmare (which we have foolishly called our wake state), to look around and see our home.

Suddenly by the speaking of the right words you will find that you are not teaching school, not running engines, not arguing law points, not translating hieroglyphics, not fighting monopolies or making them — no, you are awake at home.

*"Oh, Such a home!*

*'Tis there that thou'lt never remember*

*When from earth thy proud soul is set free.*

*That cold chilling winds of December*

*Stole all thy companions from thee."*

No. Paul told people to awake. David said he should be satisfied when he should awake. Paul wished the people of the past had been mindful of the country from whence they came out.

Hosea said, "Take with you words and return unto your God." Note your God. Paul did not feel the necessity of himself being mindful of the country from when he came out.

We will not split the rock that foundered Paul. Let us remember the country whence we came out. We will speak vehemently with the hot fervor of joy at being told that words will waken us to see what this kingdom is to which we are so asleep.

In philosophy we are told that whenever in our sleep we dream that we sleep or dream, we are dreaming, that then we are on the point of awakening. So now that we dream that we dream or are told that this is all a nightmare reminder of our home, we must be near awakening.

And that is what all the religionists and astronomers and geologists are trying to stammer about when they tell about the coming end of the world.

According to the gospel, Jesus Christ was supremely awake and is now awake. And as children and grown men and women have to be awakened out of the palsying nightmares, so Jesus Christ awakens us with His words if we speak them. Strange about it that we must speak His words ourselves. It is just as the mother cannot hold the child's eyes open, but it must open its own eyes, that Jesus Christ tells us, "Keep my words." Whoever realizes this, to him is "the arm of the Lord revealed."

If it is the law of health that the sick woman or man must say positively, "I am well," before he sees himself well, you can see why it is that we must declare ourselves wide awake and not dreaming in order to see our good that lies here. Isaiah insists that the doctrine of truth will "have no form or comeliness."

Some people do not like music; some people do not like paintings; some people do not like sculpture; some people do not like to be told the truth about the power of their own thoughts to get them into scrapes and to get them out of them. They do not see what majesty and dignity that confers upon us, and how kingly we reign over our realm of ideas. It is the law of mind that if we refuse to think certain thoughts we shall never see certain kinds of people. It is the law of mind as related to life that if we positively refuse to think certain thoughts we shall never experience certain conditions of body. It lies in the power of mind as related to life experiences that if we choose we can shut down squarely on thinking such thoughts as are simply shiftless and frivolous and only the rehearsal in memory of some past experience far from ennobling. It is a good plan to shut down on them, for they bring around us their own kinds of people and conditions.

You will be surprised how speedily a certain class of people and conditions will drop out of your life when you stop thinking certain thoughts which they personify. The early morning is said to be the time when the mind is most efficient to cut off useless branches and dead sticks by speaking silently, "I hereby cast out of my mind all such thoughts as have kept me from healthy judgment and prosperity." Then give the mind the good tonic of a strong statement like, "I am sound in health, able in judgment and satisfied with prosperity."

Now, Isaiah herein proceeds to tell us that the Lord laid upon Jesus Christ the iniquity of us all. That was true in this sense, viz., that He took the cup of our experience, which we have forced upon ourselves by imaginations, and tasted it to see what it is best for us to do under such circumstances. He has left the word that it is to be refused as the cup of nothingness.

It is no use for you to bear poverty. You can say positively, "I refuse to be poor, I refuse the cup of poverty. Jesus Christ told me that there is enough and to spare and God is my bountiful supply from this time on."

It is no use for you to cry over anything that has happened to you. Refuse the cup. It is all a nightmare. You do not need to bear anything. It is sheer nonsense for you to get down on your knees and ask God to help you bear what you were never made to bear. You can be noble and good and powerful and wise without suffering for it. It is better to cure a tumor than to carry it around with you. So it is better to dissolve a grief in the cleansing acids of right words than to lug it around.

Martyrdom is only the belief that it is pleasing to God to have us suffer. What kind of a God would that be who could create certain beings to suffer into strength? It is not any use to try to make even the meekest of us believe in and adore such a being. If Jesus Christ chose to go through all our experiences in order to tell us what to do, we will love and bless and obey Him, both as principle and demonstration of principle (which means a right-living character). In this sense only did the Lord lay on Him our iniquities. We can all choose our own thoughts, and thus choose our own companionships, such as those thoughts attract. It is very common for very gently, courageous girls, especially school-teachers, to think very depressing thoughts, and then wonder why they are so shut off from everything they would like to have. Cut off the depressing thoughts and spend every instant you can get deliberately refusing the cup of trouble, deprivation, pain, and announcing your God-given rights.

Jesus Christ felt called upon to test everything and let us see for ourselves that the whole material world is under us, not over us, nor in our arms. You will see by this 53rd chapter of Isaiah that there was nothing of suffering which we dream of in this silly nightmare that He did not test.

It is told that God hath given Him a Name above every name. That Name is the quickening principle — the awakening power. You are privileged to do with the Name as you please, but it is very evident that it means all that you wish to have and to know concentrated. Now, because the science of satisfactory living is so simple do not turn away from it. The more simple the machinery the greater its executive power. It is written that at the name of Jesus everything shall bow. If this word be in our mind this power will be in our life. We shall be surprised when we wake up to find how simple the law of masterful success is. And there is no doubt about everything depending upon a state of mind, as there is no doubt about a state of mind being induced by words or thoughts.

We often wonder why a small deformed-appearing man has such great powers. It is because he suddenly betook himself to some new way of thinking. Agesilaus II, King of Sparta, was deformed, short of stature and lame, yet he was a brilliant general. In his 18th year he went to assist the Egyptians against the Persians. He made such a poor appearance that the King of Egypt refused his alliance. Of course the King of Egypt was defeated.

There is a story of a man who had been told that the philosopher's stone was in a pile of stones, and he began to examine them throwing them away one by one after examining them. He got so in the habit of throwing them away that he got careless in his examinations and carelessly threw away the philosopher's stone with the rest. As he threw them into the sea, he never could reclaim them and lost his chance. Here is a doctrine that is the true philosopher's stone. It is the only doctrine on the face of the earth that has any practical efficiency. But it has nobody and nothing of riches or fame or name to gather its adherents with. This is exactly according to prophecy. This is therefore something to commend it, as the reigning religions have all these things on their side. Yet can you not see how^ the silent forces of its great truths are permeating, overturning, changing dynasties, religions, political, ethical?

It is one of the denials which every mind should make for its own advancement into its greatest power that it holds no prejudice of any kind. Prejudice for or prejudice against anybody or anything in all the world.

The grand jury disposed of the case of Charles Wesley in the time of an Irish mob by the following verdict: "We find Charles Wesley to be a person of ill fame, a vagabond, and a common disturber of his Majesty's peace; and we pray that he may be transported." How much do you think Homer got for his Iliad or Dante for his Paradise?

According to this prophecy of Isaiah, this is exactly the verdict people will make while the greatest doctrine ever enunciated is being taught by those who see its truth and its majesty and are willing to stand by till it demonstrates itself. They shall see of their travail and be satisfied. They shall see that it is greatly worth while to say, "I am not prejudiced for or against anybody or anything in all the world, I am satisfied with the truth of God." For they shall see that state of mind is like a clear transparency through which the Redeemer's healing light shall stream.

*"This is the dawn of noble faith,*

*The day doth follow soon.*

*When hope can breathe with freer breath,*

*For night is lost in noon."*

*January 31, 1892*

# Lesson VI

## TRUE IDEAL OF GOD

*Isaiah 55:1-13*

*"Ho, everyone that thirsteth,"* writes Isaiah. He knows enough of mind to know how it hungers and thirsts all the time for sustaining ideas.

And if he knows anything he knows that an idea which will refresh and satisfy one mind will just be brackish drink and husks for another. So when he is speaking of those waters that will quench the thirst of everybody, old and young, rich and poor alike, he must mean a different kind of waters from the ideas then being taught among men even in the schools of the prophets of Israel.

Moses had been taught years and years before Isaiah that man himself is *the "I AM THAT I AM."* David had taught the God-nature of humanity. *"I said ye are gods."* It has been running in the minds of many that as with the forward the Lord had shown Himself forward, and with the merciful had shown mercy; that there was therefore no God at all except as we should imagine one, and therefore that there is no God. It had been strongly intimated as practical doctrine what Isaiah had written in his 41st Chapter that *"We are all nothing and our works are nothing."* Therefore there is nothing at all. Again, many had practiced cold, hunger, nakedness, self-tortures, hoping to find the nature of things that they might satisfy their thirst for knowledge of what is the true way to be masters of human destiny and not slaves to it.

None of these ways of believing or performing had quenched the thirst or satisfied the hunger of anybody. Isaiah believed there was a way to get our thirst quenched, however, just as Abraham and Moses and the Egyptians and Brahmins had been believing for thousands of years. Some called this strange and unceasing hunger the call of the wick of life for oil. What the oil was that would keep the life-wick burning they could not really settle, but they finally concluded that it was the call of the mind for truth. So they practiced telling that all is God and there is no God. They practiced telling that we are all and we are nothing. They practiced telling of the interior spirits that keep record of our actions and motives as long as we live, one keeping record of the good motives and actions and the other of the not good actions and motives.

Still the hunger and the thirst kept on, and have kept on ever since.

A prophet used to be one who kept his mind on things not perceptible to the senses; and he every now and then uttered absolute truth along some line without at all realizing what he was saying. Then he wrought some miracle by what he said. Trying again to work the miracle by using the same words he would find that they would not work and then he gave up the effort to do his work by those words.

If you should go into a room, as Edward Irving did where a boy was supposed to be dying, and should cause him to spring to life again by saying, "My boy, God loves you," you might be chagrined to find that the next case would not pay the slightest attention to your words.

It ought to be of great importance to you what cured the boy in the first case, and then, of course, you would readily know why the next one did not respond. You would not have to find out by study why the second did not recover, but you would turn your attention to why and how the first one responded. Here Isaiah utters a profounder truth than has been written down, *"Expede Herculem"*. That is, if you see a foot of Hercules how can you help judging of his whole stature?

Here when Isaiah tells us that he can have no hunger and thirst of mind satisfied at this wonderful spring "without money and without price," he means first that we need not slay lambs and young bullocks hoping to get any satisfaction from a propitiated God of supply. He means also that there are no works we can do that will earn us favor with the first cause of good bounty. He means that there are no thanksgivings we can offer, no praises that we may utter, no faith we can give the Source of every blessing hoping to buy satisfaction thereby.

If one thing won't buy us any favor with Goodness, nothing will.

Isaiah rose on the wings of a mighty truth here and spoke of the Divine supply as now at hand, not to be cajoled or bought off or propitiated by anything we can do.

What a lovely Being this is whom Isaiah brings near! He already is able and ready to provide us with all things without our praising Him, hoping by praise to cajole Him. He gives us bountifully of what will feed and delight us without our begging, hoping by such gyrations of mind to please and flatter Him into rewarding us. He does not demand of us the exercise of a great faith in Him before His goodness will vouchsafe any manifestation of itself.

No, the true God is your highest ideal of supreme goodness. Spread out boldly with your words what you think the best kind of a God would do and there you have what is true of God.

Why haven't you got the gifts of the true God?

Why, we always have the gifts of that God we have described. The gifts of the true God are here. We may have them without money and without price. When you have described the untrue God you must get untrue conditions. The true God folds us around with exactly the life we like. When poverty strikes you it is not what the true God sent, but only what your former description of God has brought around you. Therefore you ought to say, "My God never sends poverty or trouble to anyone; my God supplies all my needs." This last affirmation was one that David used.

But there is a higher ideal of God than one who supplies needs. The higher ideal is of One who never lets anybody or anything need anything. There is even a higher ideal of God than of One who never lets anybody or anything need anything. The higher ideal is of One who never permitted anybody or anything to ever imagine a need.

Yet there is a still higher ideal of God than even that; it is of One who shows us all without our paying any price of praising Him or trusting Him that we are here and now safe at home in our Father's and Mother's house with the fair hills of Paradise in full sight.

Our highest ideal of God is of supreme, generous, universal, bounty, goodness, love, bliss.

Is this, then, the highest? Yes. How have we found out that it is by the description of the true God that we see the true God? By reading the lessons in Isaiah. But what illuminated our minds to see these underlying lessons? Holding the name Jesus Christ.

What is it to hold this name in our heart? Simply to speak it silently with the mind. But is not that ridiculous gymnastics? No. By knowing the nature of mind we see how much more potent with power over our life experiences some words are than others, and it is proven as an actual result that holding this name steadily illuminates the mind to know new statements of truth and to increase in strength and power and judgment. The Name means demonstration in daily life of the power and presence of the true God.

Holding the name teaches you that you need not say that you yield to the will of an imaginary God who is said to be capable of sending pain and affliction and poverty into your lot or into anybody's lot. Holding the Name causes you to see that in truth it is just as much idolatry to lay down your praises upon the altar, or your thanks, or your will, or anything, expecting to earn any favors by such offsprings, as it is to offer young lambs or doves.

You are one with the true God by describing Him, and praise and thanks and will and faith are then natural expressions of your delight. Here Isaiah tells how surely all the words that go forth out of his mouth shall prosper in the thing whereunto they are sent. But he has shown already that the thoughts we have been holding have been lower ideals than we need to have held and prosperity is the thing which we please to see prospered will only be manifest by our stating high ideals.

As to the demonstration of God with us we need only to say to the unhappy woman, "My God does not allow you to be unhappy. My God makes you supremely glad with the bounty of His goodness." We need not watch her to see if her state of mind changes. We may chase ourselves up closer than that and say, "My God does not expect me to watch to see if He is Good." According to this lesson of Isaiah we have not given our God credit for common honor.

"As the Heavens are higher than the earth, so are my thoughts higher than your thoughts." So we will describe a Good Being without human foibles or characteristics.

All these lessons carefully noted will discover to you what is called in this chapter "fatness." That is, some one of them has healing instruction for your mind which will take you right out of the place which you do not like and set you down into the place which you do like. It is intended for you that you should be doing what pleases you every minute. There is not a single tramp on the streets who has not the same ideal of God that you have if you push him step by step to tell it. Expressing it would please him.

There is not a convict or pampered prince but what has the same ideal you have. He who has covered up his ideal with many imaginations is acting basely to show how he has covered his ideal of God. But it is all there. Let him express it and be satisfied with bliss.

The same is true of everything. There is a region of the mind that knows all things. All language is understood by you already.

Lift off the rubbish and let the spring of your knowledge burst forth. Get in league with your own nature: "Thou shalt be in league with the stones of the field."

So here the lesson teaches that by a certain procedure every mind that is thirsting and hungering for wine and meat that will satisfy can find the spring of enchanting liquids and delightful viands somewhere in his own nature, in his own mind.

This procedure has been hinted at and touched upon in its various steps by every religion and by every age, but all the steps have not been given till now.

And there is so much rubbish of false notions covering the beautiful message that is meant for us alone that we have to refuse everything we have ever been taught and begin over again like little children to think what is true.

Each religion has some gem of truth in its bosom. So we must not hold any accusation against any religion. Each man and each woman is sent forth with some divine motive, and so we cannot accuse them of anything because that shows at once that we are not thinking of the divine motive of their being but are only thinking upon the nonsense that shadows them.

It is ceasing from accusation that is lifting off rubbish.

*"Swing to the right and the left,*

*Gates of sorrow and pain,*

*Let the glory of truth and her peace*

*Over earth's children reign."*

The highest wisdom of Greece was expressed in the words, "Know thyself." In the oldest religious philosophy of the world, viz., the Vedanta, the highest instruction is, "Know thyself." That which you are already within your own self is that which is your own delight. That which you are already within your own self is the divine purpose which sent you forth. If you will chase that purpose up face to face with itself you will have uncovered the true God. Suppose you find that you are working today for money? For what purpose do you want money? For easier, more pleasant living. But why do you want easier, more pleasant living? So as to be free from pain of any kind to the body. But why do you want to be free from pain of body? Because I do not like it. But why do you not like it? Because it is not my nature to like it.

There you are, face to face with your nature which you find is opposed to pain. With what does your nature feel like and dislike? With the mind. There you are, face to face with your own mind, which is exactly like everybody else's mind in the universe. It is the universal mind. And the universal mind is omnipresent mind opposed to pain. Thus God is not the giver of pain, but the opposer of pain.

*"As I live, saith the Lord, I know the thoughts that I think toward you, thoughts of peace and not of evil." "Why have ye made the heart of the righteous sad whom I have not made sad? saith the Lord."* Therefore all imaginations of pain of any kind as sent by God or pleasing to God are pure nonsense. They are accusations against God and not truth of God.

John, the Revelator, saw the time when the red dragon or the accuser should be destroyed by the testimony of the saints. Just testimony of your own mind at its starting point is sufficient to put you to drinking this wonderful water.

It seems there is no slaying, no ending of that opposition to pain within your mind and all mind. It is God himself.

There have been quite a number of miracles wrought for the planet by some strong minds knowing the truth. One miracle has been that those who believe in the pain of the world as permitted to exist by some mysterious inefficiency of Jehovah have felt the stir of their own opposition to pain, and have actually gone to work to shut up some hard actions that have brought pain. They have waged war on some places where pain was made.

Those who did not believe that pain of any kind is forced upon us by the true God were the instigators of the actions against pain by those who believe that the true God originated pain.

They are very young in their instigations against the accusers of God — or very young in their convictions that God is opposed to pain, but the growth of their strength is marvelous, and the places where pain is going on are soon to feel the same revulsions against what is not originated by the true God as the best of thinkers.

For mind is one and he who thinks truth stirs all minds to think truth. "Think truly, and thy thoughts will the world's famine feed." "Ho, everyone that thirsteth." "Buy satisfying powers without price." "My thoughts are higher than your thoughts," and "my word shall prosper in that which I please;" therefore "seek ye the Lord while He is near," for the words of God are the joy of every heart.

The most cogent instruction conveyed esoterically here in this 55th chapter of Isaiah is that the nature of every mind is opposed to evil of any kind. That the expression of this nature is feeding and watering to the mind. That there is nothing this nature, common to all minds alike, does not know. That what is called genius along any line is simply the uncovering of some one word against limitation. That genius along every line is the birthright of every creature. That genius along every line may be demonstrated by describing the true God.

That holding the name Jesus Christ teaches new powers, new faculties, true ways of uncovering the brilliant possibilities of each mind by a short, easy method.

*"My yoke is easy and my burden is light."* That knowing all this sets those who still believe God is in league with evil by permitting it, to squirming and struggling to stop it; for if they believe in it they must work in it, *"Let the dead bury the dead."* That it is better to know the true God and not have to fight than to imagine one and fight like heroes.

*"The South winds are quick witted,*

*The schools are sad and slow,*

*The masters quite omitted*

*The love we care to know."*

The end of all that the senses cognize is at hand, *"Arise, let us go hence."*

February 7, 1892

# Lesson VII

# HEAVEN AROUND US

*Jeremiah 31:14-37*

This lesson is from Jeremiah, Chapter 31. It explains the life of man under law and the life of man under grace, "The law was given by Moses, but grace and truth came by Jesus Christ." When we come to appreciate the difference between what are our experiences while subject to the law of matter and its mind, and our experiences while under the gospel of Spirit we see the work which Jesus Christ wrought, "Christ has redeemed us from the curse of the law."

This lesson explains two other points, namely, what it means to acknowledge God in all our ways, and what it means to *"look unto Me and be ye saved all the ends of the earth."*

When shrinking, timid, young Jeremiah hears the truth of God he feels that he cannot preach it, so he says, "I am only a child." Then the God rises within him and sternly commands, "say not thou I am a child; see, I have this day set thee over the nations and over the kingdoms." This command to Jeremiah is commanded to all who have heard that their substance is God, their life is God, and their intelligence is God. It completely takes away from us the pleasing delusion, "I am only a child who is lying on the bosom of Infinite love," and puts it in its place, "I am infinite self-responsibility."

The command to look unto God in all words and ways is the same as "Stand thou upright on thy feet." and understand the atonement! Or that thou and God are one and inseparable spirit. For we understand distinctly that only spirit can look at spirit and thus as we are of the same substance God is, we are looking at our own substance when we realize salvation. It is another way of putting the doctrine that to know ourselves is the highest knowledge.

Jesus Christ found men under both the physical and metaphysical law. That is, He found them looking at matter as reigning over them, and also at carnal mind as reigning over them. He ignored both the physical and metaphysical bondage of mankind, and showed them free grace. That nobody has ever accepted the freedom He offered, so they also are free as He was, does not make His office less.

He found them believing that they must wait for summer and winter, seedtime and harvest, grinding and baking, for their bread. He showed them that this was not necessary, and increased five loaves without any material procedure into quite enough to feed 5,000 men, besides women and children. *"I have meat to eat that ye know not of;"* we do not need to spawn and hook fish, He explained, and He ignored physical law and multiplied fish with the bread.

He showed that no man with cataracts on his eyes need go into a dark room and lie waiting, after a skillful operation by some sharp instrument in the hands of a surgeon, in order to see clearly. A word is quite sufficient. "I came to bring recovery of sight to the blind" by the gospel.

He ignored grape culture, and yet produced reviving wines. "Buy wine, without money and without price," by turning water into wine at your word was His instruction. He spoke to the gold in the fish, and it precipitated at once. He proved that it is not by might or power of horseman or steel that one is best defended from earthly foes, by causing the officers and soldiers to fall backward and upon their faces at sight of Him.

There is something surpassing all things in one who holds true ideas. The name of Jesus Christ when held hard in mind will quicken all our powers — quicken our signs of greatness. At the information of the seventh angel in Revelation, that the kingdoms of the world were to become the kingdoms of Christ, the four and twenty elders fell down on their faces. These four and twenty elders represent the statements of the law under which mankind has had its neck — the twelve laws of matter and the twelve laws of mind. You will find these laws as related to human experience, put together in what are called the twelve lessons on Christian Science.

But while they are very good to announce God with, they are finally to fall down on their faces and yield the point that free grace is divinely more tender than salvation earned by obedience to law. The seventh angel is the seventh definite teaching concerning God. The seventh angel is now sounding. There is no uncertain sound in this last doctrine of God. You will find a perfect description of this hour and the way this teaching of the truth that God is all and there is none else, in Chapter 11 of Revelation, commencing at verse 15.

There you will see that heaven is all around us. We are the temple of God. We open our mind to speak truth no matter what seems opposed to us, and we find that on our heart is written the covenant with God whereby we are to never hear of, or know trouble any more forever, and that all the miserable people on the earth are really waiting for the truth concerning God to be told them.

This truth is written within them, but what is called religious teachings have hidden their heaven and their covenant with God.

Robinson Crusoe felt that he must teach Friday about God and the devil so as to be doing his Christian duty by that child of nature. Friday understood readily about God, but why the good God who was so strong didn't "kill the debble" was a mystery that confused him. This convinced Crusoe that a supernatural and revealed religion was absolutely necessary to salvation.

The supernatural and revealed religion that tells of the Supreme Good as authorizing or permitting evil is that which closes the temple of mind. Now the seventh angel sounds and we hear that that was not and never will be true. Jesus Christ annulled the metaphysical laws as utterly as the physical. The metaphysical law is *that "He that leadeth into captivity shall be led captive, and he that Killeth with the sword shall be killed by the sword." "This was the patience and the faith of the saints."* But there is to be no sword — no venge*ance;* mankind are all to be told the truth. *"The truth shall make them free."*

Under the law of metaphysics, "for the lightest word thou shalt give account." Under this law the physical body registers all the mistakes of the mind in disease, sickness, poverty, pain. But with the knowledge of Christ or Truth we are set free from the results of words and thoughts. To accept the freedom of Christ is to accept immunity from the law of cause and effect.

All the lessons in law fall on their faces with gratitude that the highest truth has taken to itself its great power and will now reign. This law of cause and effect has for its teaching many strong clauses which have made people almost afraid to think and to speak. Under this law to say to a child, "Poor little thing," is to cause it to grow up poor in purse, poor in flesh, and timid and shrinking. Under this law if one gets a counterfeit dollar into his possession by mistake he knows he must have sometime let somebody pay him a few cents too much change and did not rectify it. The few cents have come back with interest — out of hand. Under this law every blind person we meet is the outpicturing of some refusal on our part to see the justice done ourselves or somebody else. Under this law we have Karma, that is, repeated returns of the consequences of our deeds and thoughts.

According to early metaphysics it was considered unpardonable ignorance not to be able to quickly detect the errors that had caused the troubles suffered by people. But "Christ redeemed us from the curse of the law." *"Let no fruit grow on thee,"* He said to the most vigorous and flourishing signs of the powers of evil. For you must bear in mind that He was giving a lesson in the annulling power of the gospel when He blasted the vigorous fig tree.

*"Thy sins be forgiven thee"* — this is the gospel. It is possible for us all to say and have the words come true, I refuse the consequences of my past words and thoughts. I do not live under the law but under the gospel. I am free from the law.

Under the gospel there is no heredity of body or mind. Under grace there is no deception or consequences of deception. Under grace there is no discord. Under grace there is no foolishness or ignorance or consequences of foolishness or ignorance. Under grace there is no death, there is illumination. One can keep under the law as long as he pleases, and one can accept grace when one pleases.

There is a mystery or secret about Jesus Christ and free grace which cannot be communicated. It will come by speaking the name Jesus Christ. Nobody can tell the way he feels when he sees himself no longer under the law but under grace. He can only say that the name is the "name overall victorious."

The atonement here taught by this chapter where God and His people are One is sometimes expressed by "seeing God." We must know that we are exactly what we see. To see is to understand. To understand God is to be God. This is written in the heart.

*"Look unto Me"* is a command that has almost escaped the notice of mankind when studying Scriptures. There is a mystery about looking steadily at anything that has escaped the mention of philosophers.

The Germans of ancient times used to heal by looking straight at their patients and saying, "God looks you quite away." They thus really looked straight past the appearance to the reality or spiritual man and caused it to stand forth as health. It was their own spirit looking at the spirit of the other and the twain being one, that which was nothing fell away. Great healing was wrought this way.

It has been found out that by looking at some one proposition of any language anybody can catch the clew to the language and without study know it by the instruction of spirit. Heaven is around us. There is only heaven around us. To look steadily at anything around is really to be looking into heaven. Keep on looking until it is plain.

A young man was told that certain envelopes in a circle of sealed envelopes contained money. There was no clew to those with money enclosed and those without money. But he found out every one that contained money by looking at them a long time, till those containing what he wished for seemed to have a mark on them and be the only envelopes there at all. See what small issues confirm great ones.

All that you can ask is lying near you, "Look and see." There is a substance within us akin to every other substance. There is a divining rod or touchstone within us to draw all that we can think of.

The Chinese have a habit of placing a shining stone on a high stand in the middle of the room and sitting down in a circle and gazing steadfastly up at the stone, expecting it to hand them down blessings. They who look steadily enough always get their blessings. There is a cathedral in the East where there hangs in a darkened room a picture of the Virgin Mary. The sunlight strikes across her face, and all the lame, palsied, and deaf go there and gaze steadfastly up into her face. There have been thousands healed by thus looking at the picture till the symbol quite faded and the healing spirit smiled answers.

All obstacles may be looked away from the spirit of success. All obstacles may be looked away from the bounty of God. It is the Spirit bearing witness with our spirit that we are one. This witness of spirit with spirit is atonement — one *metis* or one mind.

The highest good your heart can conceive is the good that lies waiting to bless you. It is going to be utterly impossible for combinations of men or single men to keep the success and the substance of other men from them as it is impossible to keep God from God, with the catching sight of truth.

Drop your supernatural and revealed religion, so-called, and open your mind to describe what you think is bliss. Look all the obstacles away from your idea of bliss.

That which is written within you is truth; that which you have been told is false. The kingdom of heaven is at hand, not trouble and despair and misery; these are the fruits of revealed or supposed religion. Look past them as you would look past a mask hiding the beautiful face of your child. You can make the sun look pale and murky at noonday with a piece of smoked glass. Take away the glass and there is the sunshine. Take away your former religion, which had so much about death and sorrow and sin, and see what is true.

See! Look! Thou and God are one and inseparable. This is truth. No other truth will work miracles. If you know all about the stars and their orbits, can bind the Pleiades and loose the bonds of Orion, it is not worth while unless your heart has opened and recognized truth.

Read over this 31st chapter of Jeremiah and see how all the ordinances of the earth are made naught by the gospel of grace. Read over the last verses of Chapter 11, Revelations, and see how these times confirm the prophecies. Realize what is now being taught and see if you are among the voices of opposition, the thunders and lightnings of holding on to the old ways of thinking, or among the bold and redeemed and fearless under grace.

Remember that what is true of principle is true of practice. Practice and principle are one. If you cannot prove that God is your provider, your defense, your health, your inspiration, 'what comfort can you be getting out of your religion?

*These things are not waiting for proof till after death. They are now. Look! Look around you. Look steadily. The kingdom of heaven folds you round. There is no law under which you need keep your neck. You are free under grace.* "I will forgive thine iniquity and remember thine sin no more."

"I will watch over them to build and to plant." "Look unto Me!" "I am nigh *thee."* All things are passing — God never changeth.

I fill those objects near thee. I fill those circumstances near thee. Look steadfastly. I will reveal myself to the steadfast seeker. *"I in thee and thou in Me." "Is there any beside Me? May, I know not any."*

"Say not thou, 'I am a child' — see! I set thee this day over the nations and over the kingdoms." Take thine inheritance. The law is under thy feet. *"Old things are forgotten." "All things are made new."*

*February 14, 1892*

# Lesson VIII

# BUT ONE SUBSTANCE

*Jeremiah 36:19-31*

This burning of the prophecies of Jeremiah by Jehoiakim, King of Judah, brings to remembrance the old Latin proverb, *Qui unit decipi, decpiatur*, which means, "Let him who wishes to be deceived, be deceived."

Jeremiah had written to Jehoiakim that there were two ways for him to save Judah from destruction — one was by yielding to Babylon which, though under the horizon of power (that is, not apparently the coming power), was yet going to conquer all nations; and the other way was to call a great assembly to prayer as Hezekiah had done about a hundred years before.

There were no signs of Babylon attacking Jerusalem and Jehoiakim burned the roll containing the advices of Jeremiah. They seemed to him nonsense. As a king he felt that his words and actions must be worth more than a prophet's impressions, and he felt a pompous certainty that he knew his own business best. At any rate he wanted not to believe Jeremiah, and it was his choice to set up a scheme defying the defense of prayer and the defense of horsemen. Babylon stood for the intelligence of worldliness, and prayer stood for the intelligence of spirit. Jehoiakim did not want to use intelligence in being safe. He just wanted to be safe. So he burned the instructions of Jeremiah. It was as though a man should burn the bill of goods purchased by him at some store, thinking that would end the matter.

You have heard before that "the letter killeth." The kingdom of Judah stood for the letter of truth. It lived longer than the kingdom of Israel, which stood for the feeling of truth. Hoshea, the last king of Israel, was weak and irresolute, though good enough, and was overthrown.

That is the way with all feelings not headed by judgment. Feeling causes people to do things because they like or dislike. They love somebody sentimentally, and no matter what that one would do in a position of trust they put him there. They dislike somebody and no matter what his fitness for a position they would not let him have it. So their kingdom wanes. All things get to running intolerably, like the watch which the owner cannot use and the watchmaker cannot see why it will not run when its works are so perfect, till they find its balance-wheel is magnetized.

Judah stood for the word or letter which also kills itself. When once word and feeling are married they give good judgment. Jehoiakim said exactly the right words but he said them without intelligence. He was like one who says that the child with typhoid fever has nothing at all the matter, because he never saw such a case and hasn't the remotest idea what he has to meet, but has heard the scientific statement that all claims of evil are nothing at all. So he says the words and goes to sleep to wake and find the child dead, and himself condemned for criminal carelessness. As Jehoiakim refused both the intelligence of spirit and the intelligence of armies he was wound up. Zeal without judgment, and word without judgment, are equally self-destructive. Both Jeremiah and Jehoiakim believed in law and so both had to fulfill the law exactly as it demands. Of course, there is a higher than law, under whose wings one can throw himself and come out unscathed, but neither of these men recognized this in a way to save their kingdom.

Jeremiah did not appeal to the highest nature of Jehoiakim; Jehoiakim did not permit it to speak.

We get the rewards of that principle we serve. If we believe in Spanish flies as the cure for neuralgia we must use Spanish flies till they fail us. Jeremiah believed that the children of Judah had done evil and so, of course, he expected evil to reward them. It was Hahnemann's *similia similbus curantur* (Like things are cured by like – the foundation of homeopathy.).

It goes with the belief in the law of evil that punishment must follow offenses, and what sort of seeds we sow those we reap. There is an intelligent repudiation of this law which will set anybody free from the consequences of his own past foolish or ignorant words.

But neither the Israelite nor the Judahite performs intelligently except when turning his annulling words toward God. Jeremiah, Isaiah, Stephen, Guyon, were all martyrs to their belief in evil as belonging to them. Looking into material things for their own sake, they will be sure to give you their kind of fruitage.

The man who invented the telescope was put into a dungeon. The man who constructed the microscope starved to death. They had no intelligence of life. If you feed a man who tells you he is starving while you know he is not honest, yet your principle of conduct compels you to do kindly by him, he will be the means of bringing you some good in some way unintentionally. If you feel tenderness and mercy some way he will get you a merciful return for your action.

*"Say never affection was wasted.*

*Affection never was wasted.*

*If it enrich not the heart of another,*

*Its waters returning back to their fountains*

*Shall fill them full of refreshment.*

*That which the fountain rejected*

*Returning again to the fountain."*

Probably the point that will strike the intelligent metaphysician as strongest in this lesson is that there are two ways of denying evil and matter: one intelligently, and the other blindly.

One of the first propositions of Christian doctrine is that there is but one substance filling all space, all places, all things. There is but one substance.

As there can be but one omnipresence of cause this substance everywhere present is God. God is good. Thus all is good. Then there follows the necessary negation to such a promise, viz., then there is no evil.

The intelligent acceptance of this reasoning has the most straightening and purifying effect upon character. All appetites, passions, tempers, diseases stop as if by magic. The blind acceptance of this reasoning causes people to act exactly like Jehoiakim. Whatever appetite or passion or temper they had before they now say it is good because there is no evil. Now that one little turn of metaphysics contains all the law and the gospel. It makes all the difference between intelligence and ignorance, light and darkness.

The one who says his conduct is good when it is manifestly bad is as much a believer in evil and will take as much punishment for evil as he did before he spoke the words. For demonstration is the accompaniment of truth understood. Whoever says there is no evil because good is all will show forth good only, else he does not believe a word he is saying. He really is thinking that evil is all. So he shows forth what he is thinking. It is just the same with sickness. Unless we show out health at once when we say there is no sickness because God is all and God cannot be sick, of course we are believing within our minds that sickness is real. It is as plain as the sunshine what we believe in. We show it out.

Remember the words of Jesus, *"According to thy faith be it unto thee."* A blind woman believed that she could see, no matter how she had been deceived by teachings about matter and evil, because God had made her. She held onto her conviction that if God made her perfect she really must be perfect, until suddenly her sight came as clear as crystal. There have been many such cases where the conviction was based on intelligent reasoning, which suddenly showed forth in health, even in straightening crooked bones.

Truth understood is as straightening to character as to bones.

This is Christian science. We do not understand the science unless we demonstrate it, so Jehoiakim had no intelligent conception of his denial of evil and matter. It is intelligence that is God. It is the word of intelligence that is God manifest.

It is here that the presence and office of Jesus Christ come in. The mind has been so accustomed to sophistries that it seems to be easy to lead even quite bright-appearing people off into byways and hedges and blind alleys. This name holds the mind to judgment and to demonstration of goodness.

It is at this point of statement that students of science halt and begin to think that it is license to evil and not power of good the science effects. Here they stop to accuse each other and to draw off from each other. Here at this juncture they have to start their reasoning over again, clinging fast to the name that stands for wholeness and goodness. At this point many sorrowful experiences face the student. He will take them into his talk and reasoning or refuse them. Here he feels he is right and everybody else in the wrong, and he refuses to let any man buy or sell save as he has "his mark on his forehead or in his right hand."

This is the place where those who choose to declare that God is not respecter of persons and has filled with His substance and power all men alike, begin to create or enter into the new heaven and the new earth, where they hunger no more, neither thirst any more, and their joy no man can take away. Here is where intelligence seems to fail and one has to rise and announce that intelligence is God, and as God cannot fail so intelligence cannot fail. Here is where provisions seem to stop and one has to rise and announce that as God cannot be cut off, so support cannot be cut off or stop.

There are times when the mind has to see only one side of the question on intelligent principle. There have been many examples of this sudden rising to announce truth from the Jesus Christ standpoint and the effect has been wonderful.

It is not sentimental wishing and it is not simple denial and affirmation that work when the forces of the claims of evil meet the scientific statements. It is honest conviction. And "conviction is not properly speaking conviction till it develops itself into action."

Looking over the young people just starting out upon the voyage of human experience, strict science says to each one: "Rise, when sorrow, pain, disappointment come to you, and say with all the force of your mind, I refuse them! Jesus Christ told me not to experience this and I will not."

Whatever came knocking at your door will fall away from your lot. The next test will be easier. And so you will demonstrate God in life. You will be a living glory to the world. You will bring the new heaven and the new earth, and the former will be forgotten. Look at the gray-haired, deeply wrinkled faces of the people you meet. What aged them thus? Drinking the cup of sorrow, pain, disappointment, supposing that it was the common lot of mankind. Never. If they had refused to feel badly, refused to think of the pain, sorrow, and disappointment, because God never intended it for them, they would be beautiful as the archangels, living lights to the dark places, healing to the nations.

Now that the science of good has come we will accept the glorious offering.

There is only one beauty, health, bounty, buoyant youth in truth.

The letter of denial must be united to the conviction that it is a truth. The feeling of denial must be united to do the word of right reasoning. Then we enter upon our rightful kind of life. It is just beginning to be proven how foolish the sufferings of good people have been through mistaken notions of God's intentions towards them.

*February 21, 1892*

# Lesson IX

## JUSTICE OF JEHOVAH

*Jeremiah 37:11-21*

This lesson suggests two points that have been brought up again and again, but are ever good to be brought to mind. The first is that, so far as our own self is concerned, in this training process we must take the position of non-resistance to both good and evil. The second is that in dealing with the great problem of the world, the sending forth of true words from the heart is more efficient than all the personal hand-to-hand efforts we can make.

Then, too, the lesson brings up the old, old question as to why it is that those who love God best and give life and time and heart and all things to the service of God after the highest dictates of their convictions have always been the persecuted and abused and tormented of the world.

Here it is over again, rehearsed in the imprisonment of Jeremiah on an unjust charge, made by the princes against him through spite. The siege of Babylon against Jerusalem is now raging. Zedekiah is now king over Judah. Jeremiah had foreseen it when nobody else did and warned them of the only safe course, but, being disregarded, the siege is now on.

Zedekiah means "Justice of Jehovah." There is a sure working of cause and effect on the side of human experience that has been called the justice of Jehovah. It is the way the good looks to those who believe in evil. The good does not look at all that way to those who do not believe in the reality or power of evil. This justice or logic of events is shown by the downfall of Israel and Judah.

Israel refused to lean upon spirit, and turned to Egypt for assistance. Egypt failed her. Egypt stands for materiality. The most sentimental minister must not lean upon material things to brace up his work with. Neither must the most formal one. Judah was now looking to Egypt for aid and Egypt was failing him. The minister who goes from Methodism to Congregationalism, from Congregationalism to Presbyterianism, etc., to comply with the salaries offered, is a preacher of the letter of the law and has no noble principle which will keep him from extreme poverty of health and purse and brain one of these days.

He depends on Egypt's materiality. He must look at Zedekiah's fate. He represents the minister of God who preaches the letter even though very ably and his heart is not in principle.

Jeremiah told them to yield to Chaldea, which as a lesson to ministers means, go into some work besides preaching and meditate upon what you do believe before you attempt to publicly preach God.

Of course a still higher way is to call halt and cry mightily unto principle till you are united therewith demonstrably enough to be cured and well provided for by the grace of spirit.

But Israel and Judah do not do that.

The ministers of God who preach that "the earth is the Lord's and the fullness thereof," must be careful not to give the world over to Satan in their preaching, because it shows letter and not consistent principle. We must be careful not to remark that the reward of St. Stephen for serving God was paid by the world with stones, without adding that Stephen believed in stones, else he would not be stoned. We must know that what we believe in is what we are serving. We might believe that there is a satan and that would be quite service enough to get satanic dealings. Guyon loved God and asked particularly that the usual torments and hardships and martyrdoms of God's people be given to her. She got them. But God did not send them. It is blasphemy of Divine goodness to say that Divine goodness ever sent evil. Can a sweet fountain send forth bitterness?

They who have washed their robes white are those who have spoken high, clean truth unmixed with error.

The high clean truth of God is that all evil experiences are just beliefs and not realities. He who believes in limitations will be finding limitations constantly. He who believes there is an open door as Jesus taught will find limitations broken down more and more.

People often notice that Christian scientists are limited in powers and abilities like other people. If so then they believe in limitations just as they were taught in youth and pay little heed to the actual teachings of Jesus about unlimited good. By repeated instructions we may be sure to feel all that we say and thus drop our palsied hands, lame feet, rheumatic limbs, and poor eyesight. It is our privilege. It is not by leaning on Egypt that we get our health, strength and happiness, for that has been a demonstrable failure after ages upon ages of trial thereof.

In the management of those things that seem so bad in what is called the external world we see by this lesson that more good can be wrought by thinking and speaking unadulterated truth than by physical efforts. For illustration, think of Peter in prison under Herod under strong guards and behind stone walls, with heavy chains on his hands. Could the Christians of his time hope by pounding the walls or cajoling the jailors to get Peter out?

That is exactly where millions of people are now placed by the Herod belief in poverty and trouble. By going down in the alleys and carrying flowers and salves do you touch poverty so as to cajole it out of the notion of hedging millions behind its bars? Do you pound the walls built by trouble so that they shake a bit by all that you have done with your missions? Well, that is because you do not understand the principle that leads captivity captive.

Peter kept speaking truth; so did Mary and the rest of the Christian church at home. By and by one of them spoke the very truth that had the setting-free power. This truth appeared as an angel and touching Peter the chains fell off his hands and the prison doors opened.

Truth is mighty. Elisha spoke so many noble words of truth that many angels appeared to him. Jesus had angels come and minister unto Him. Angels are true words. About two hundred years ago a priest who loved truth found that he could heal the sick by speaking certain words. Thousands whom pills and poultices and surgery and other material methods would not cure were cured by these words of truth. Maxwell, a Scotch physician, cared a great deal about healing people, and while he was thinking over the need of healing by some other way than the failing methods of materiality, he suddenly saw that the universe is filled with bright, fleet, ethereal light. All things are radiant with this light. But not unless we get into a certain state of mind can we see this light. He said we could store up a fullness of this light and pass it along over the fleet light that spins through all space, and wherever our light should shine those people would he healed no matter how far away they might be.

All things seem to be so dependent upon states of mind that it is a mystery why there has not been more notice of the effects of states of mind and the process by which to attain correct states of mind.

When you are cold clear to your marrow bone all of a sudden you feel warm. Do you know what made you warm? It was a thought you thought last week just got ready to work while you were cold. Sometimes you are tired and discouraged and suddenly are cheerful and rested. It was a sudden thought that flashed through your mind that rested you. Maybe a line of a loving old hymn. One may be hungry and suddenly not hungry. A loving word spoken to somebody else who did not appreciate it went over and lodged in the mind of the hungry one and he felt fed. "Thy words were found and I did eat them."

Now and then people wonder why the Christian scientists wear warm clothes and eat and sleep like other people if they believe there is a mental state equal to warmth, food, and rest. Christ, their teacher, told them to take no thought about eating, drinking and sleeping, but take such things as should be provided naturally according to their time and station, but to be sure to preach all the time the good word, heal the sick by their word, cast out tempers by their true words, raise the dead by their true words and then that all the rest would come to them. So they obey His orders, and they do indeed have things right and good.

You remember that He and His yoke were so easy and His burden so light that people would have one hundred fold more in this sphere of experience than before obeying Him, and that in the next higher state of mind they would not have to consult or confer about death at all.

According to this it is in no sense pleasing to Him, to have anybody shutting himself up within a cell or starving or freezing himself. Such things show foolish misunderstandings of Him and His doctrines. This lesson teaches that success in your own state of mind is best secured by an attitude of non-resistance to both good and evil.

When Jesus Christ felt the touch of the Holy Spirit and heard the voice say, *"This is My beloved Son,"* He answered never a word. When they accused Him of being a glutton and a wine-bibber, He answered nothing. *"As a sheep before her shearers is dumb so He opened not His mouth."*

But when the voice gave a noble message to Moses he shrank muttering, "What will people think of me?" When Jeremiah heard the voice giving him the great honor, he shrank murmuring, *"I can't, I'm too young."*

These both resisted the good. But when evil shows its intentions Jeremiah resisted nothing but stood back a helpless spectator of the panorama.

He thought if Judah had sinned, Judah's punishment was unavertible. This was natural effect, he said. Jesus Christ told us that that idea of eye for eye and tooth for tooth was entirely wrong, for we should not meet evil by fighting it with its own weapons. "The weapons of our warfare are not carnal but mighty through God to the pulling down of strongholds." When He said, "Resist the devil and he will flee from you," He knew how everything that claims to be bad also claims to have its own way of proceeding and thus claims its own amount and kind of intelligence. Rheumatism claims a way of its own. So does softening of the brain. So does poverty. So do all so-called bad things.

When Martin Luther threw a material inkstand at a phantom Satan he showed he did not understand scientific handling of phantoms, for this phantom was much with him afterwards. Two men were suddenly set upon by an enormous bear in a field. They were both unarmed, and when the bear began hugging one of them the other man, by that sudden flashing of the weapon of defense which every creature carries, began to talk to the bear somewhat like this, "I'm ashamed and astonished to see a great, noble bear like you spring out in this way on two men who just now have nothing to fight you with. You ought to be ashamed of such a mean action and get down at once from my friend and get you gone to your lair where you belong." That bear actually got down in a shamed way and slunk back to the forest where he came from.

A man hurt his hand between two stones, and as he felt he must support his family and could not take time to nurse a mangled hand back to health, he held the hand up and said to the pain and blood, "Now I cannot spare my hand. You must not stay with me hanging on to my hand and keeping me from doing my work. You must get right away at once."

Within a few minutes the hand was hardy enough to use.

A woman had inflammatory rheumatism coming on. She was a good Catholic, so she made the sign of the cross on her limbs several times, wetting her finger as so many of the good Catholics of the past used to do. When the pain did not stop she suddenly spoke to it as if it was a live thing saying, "Look here, now; I have done my part. I have crossed myself as many times as ought to satisfy a decent pain that it was time for it to go away. Now you do your part and get away from me to where you belong." Sure enough the pain left her at once.

Any position you take of mastery is your self-empowering to victory. In Christian science people use a reason for the hope that is in them when they name a pain or trouble to unname it by saying that its name is all there is to it.

Jeremiah had a wonderfully executive mind. He might have faced up all the horrors of Chaldean warfare and stopped them. But to him they were real, and Zedekiah's weak character was so in need of punishment that he focused to the teachings he had formally received about eye for eye and tooth for tooth. There is one thing that a strong mind generally does if it does not look well to its own independent reasoning, and that is to cohere to a prejudice. Then it speaks forth from that when its mighty possibilities are to gather a store of truth and heal all things. Poverty, trouble, warfare, injustice, may all be met by a reasonable argument, and reasoned out of the universe, as the bear was reasoned away from the man. Jeremiah saved himself from death at this siege by believing one passage of Jewish teachings, viz., "I am with thee, saith the Lord, to deliver thee." Almost all good Christians believe in a God who crowds them down into the most dreadful straits and then picks them out at the last minute. They keep forgetting that if they make up such an idol it will do so by them according to their faith.

We had better not take any preconceived teachings or strange notions to the Bible when we study it, for those preconceptions act like smoked glass before the eyes of the mind.

Jonathan Edwards got from his father a notion that the universe is nowhere save in Divine Mind, and in this mind God is holding His children over lakes of fire by threads.

A great thinker got a prejudice whereby he felt that Jesus Christ taught a lower system of morals than Juvenal, the Roman poet, who lived about 40 A.D., inasmuch as Jesus taught behaving one's self for fear of hellfire and the council, while Juvenal taught that good men love virtue for its own sake, while bad men act virtuously for fear of punishment.

Eckart, the Vicar of the Dominicans about the year 1300, got out of his study of scriptures that his greatest prayer must be to get rid of God. Maitland got out of his study of the Bible that "God is the bogie of the nurseries." Tyndall, who in 1526 distributed 150,000 Bibles over England, got the idea that he must be burned for doing good.

The Christian scientist gets out of the Scriptures that this is the day when the sun shall be darkened and the moon refuse her light for the Lord God and the Lamb are the only light we need.

Reading carefully we find that all the lights of the past fade under the glory of truth believed untrammeled by prejudices. We see that all the nations are stepping their feet into that country where there is no more pain, neither sorrow nor crying. This country where "there is no evil at all" is in the mind that looks unto truth as its light and its salvation, its defiance and its provision.

And out of the Scriptures we read that whatsoever the mind believes is true and real, that the body shall experience. Out of the Scriptures we read that when we believe what is absolutely true, then indeed is the Kingdom of Heaven come and the prisoners of human experience are set free.

*February 28, 1892*

# Lesson X

# GOD AND MAN ARE ONE

### *Jeremiah 39:1-10*

Jeremiah wrote this history. All human history is but the transcription of a dream. It never happened at all. If the circumstances and events and laws and phenomena of human experience ever did take place — ever were set going by any being — then there is no telling what may lie in wait for us after this experience and no supposing of what happened before this was set going. Also there is no possibility of admiring or loving their origin.

Strict investigation of Scripture and strict logic compels us to see that "as from a dream one awaketh," so may we arise from all this phantasmagoria now, "Now is the accepted time. Now is the day of salvation."

The "I" of every living thing is the maker of its own experiences. The "I" stands at the center of being and thinks its thoughts. All thoughts are thrown outward into forms. Thoughts that are true make substantial and enduring forms. Thoughts that are only suppositions shadow the substantial and good.

Many a thinker has felt this truth and spoken it. The best words seem to have been spoken by good physicians. This was because they were enamored of the idea of helping others.

Descartes, the French philosopher, thought that the key to the understanding of the mystery of life lay in understanding how to heal. Sir Thomas Brown said; "The severe learning of the schools shall never take from me the conviction that what we perceive with the senses only shadows some substantial realities which the sense cannot cognize."

Whoever shall learn to recall all the thoughts he has ever thought home to himself, and start them over again as truth only, without supposing anything, will find his world transformed. We do not need to see the world as we have seen it. We may learn to see it as truth expressed by thinking truth. When we think such things as this 39th Chapter of Jeremiah tells, we are not thinking truth unless we look to the esoteric significance. The esoteric meaning of all this is that by supposing what is not true we are likely to get into just such a situation as Zedekiah did. It would not be a real situation.

Nothing could make it real, but it might seem very real to us. The whole lesson may be resolved into a state of mind showing itself outwardly.

Nebuchadnezzar, King of Babylon, is our most determined belief in the reality of the world as it appears to the scholar. The scholar is always proudly certain that he knows all that the world has taught, and what has been accepted by scholars must be accepted by the church which he attends.

The letter of the church must be besieged by the school till the minister of spiritual messages cannot be listened to if his worldly education has been neglected.

Then the church runs out upon the plains of blank fear and yields the question. The single mind does the same with its thoughts. If ever you have a thought you had to study Latin or Sanscrit or Greek roots or logic in order to know highest good, you also are Zedekiah running out on the plains of blank fear. Nebuchadnezzar is after you. For the fact is you do not have to study these things at all. Jerusalem is yours. You know all things within your own mind. This is truth.

Wisdom is yours. At the center of your being you are identical with wisdom itself. This is the truth. At the center of your mind you can stand and refuse all the notions of Babylon (or the world). Always your neighbors will be exactly like those you now associate with so long as you stand at the center of your mind and suppose the things that you now do. Always you will be forgetful and inferior and depressed and snubbed, so long as you stand at the center and load and fire such suppositions as you do now.

It is your privilege never to yield a point to Babylon, but instead to dictate to Babylon. Society should not dictate to you that there is any difference among the sons and daughters of God. You should ignore such errors and transcend society with the words of truth. Babylon shall be cringing to Jerusalem. Society shall cringe like a shadow under the words, "There is neither Jew nor Gentile, Greek nor barbarian, bond nor free," in truth. It is only in error there is difference.

But then you must never forget that society is something that you make for yourself by your thoughts. You must not be led by any experience of any sort or kind to believe that by nature you are not divine. If anybody tells you that you are a miserable sinner at heart, who empowered him to tell you that and why should you believe him?

Why not stand upright at the center of mind, quite ignoring him and his words, and look into your own nature for yourself? Any yielding the point of your own central wisdom and divinity is being chased by the King of Babylon.

For the highest teaching of Babylon is that you know nothing and must be taught everything. This is not truth.

Here where it tells that the Chaldeans broke down the walls of Jerusalem you may see how your stronghold, that the "spirit shall teach you all things", must never yield the point in the first place that schools are necessary to your knowledge. This does not argue against schools, but only against dependence upon them. Self-knowledge is the knowledge of God, which is mastery of all other knowledges. If there is a way of thinking about God that has the effect of healing the sick, that is surely the true way to think about God. If there is a way to think about God that will strengthen your judgment, that is without doubt, the true way to think about God.

It is practical. Do not believe a single thing that very learned men tell you, if they show no sign of truth in their conduct or bodily states. If a man must of necessity show forth his own thoughts upon his body his thoughts must be erroneous if he has sick spells, lameness, blindness, rheumatic pains, or nervous exhaustion.

There must be some great error in the mind of that learned man who finally has softening of the brain. There must be some great mistake in that preacher's doctrine who has to recuperate from overwork. "My words are life to them that find them and health to all their flesh."

There will not be the least studying of Dante, or Goethe, or Shakespeare when it is found that their errors of mind are silently communicated to all those readers who have not been so steadied by knowing truth but that unhealthy ideas can chase them and break down the walls of their safety

(Jerusalem). There is mighty error of mind which each one of these communicates to his readers.

Many a young man and maiden has disappointed his or her friends' high hopes because they caught the infliction of the false ideas held by the brilliant authors and mighty scholars whose writings they read with delight. Every child is supremely above his books.

There is a way of teaching, or drawing forth from the wonderful love possessed by children. But nobody has learned that way so but that the walls of Jerusalem, or the beautiful gates of the child-mind are always broken down by worldly insisting upon knowledge from without. This knowledge, as all the scholars know, is constantly varying, constantly being upset. There is only one knowledge that remains eternally changeless, *Cogito, ergo sum* (I think, therefore to be. Descartes translated it into French as "I think, therefore I am.."). This is the innate knowledge of the "I Am."

Whoever can get the child to stand by his own self-conviction quite independent of any instruction whatsoever from without has the secret of education and starts the demonstration of genius. Jesus Christ would not be taught anything. "He needed not that any man should teach Him." Do you suppose that any child is different from Jesus Christ? Not at all.

If you think that any child is different from Jesus Christ you think a falsity and simply show that your walls of Jerusalem have been broken down.

Mary and Joseph showed great wisdom in letting their little Jesus have so much freedom. Of course He was not constantly told not to do this and not to do that, and He was never scolded. They knew what all parents ought to know, viz., that every child's "face always beholds the face of the Father."

In speaking forth that truth which the child always knew from the beginning, He urged upon men not ever to judge from appearances but to start judgment from right reasoning.

Right reasoning is like a wind that blows great trees down and sends the chaff flying off the earth. Right reasoning held by a few minds will blow all the errors out of the mind of humanity. Right reasoning gives the metaphysical purport of all the historic records of Scripture. And purely metaphysical reasonings dissolve all materiality, "The earth is clean dissolved."

You have heard that absolutely pure water would dissolve everything it touched. Pure reasoning is pure water. It is that pure reasoning that is now turning the steam loose over the world mind. The elements cannot help melting. If a little child should stand up and speak forth its own inner knowing, nothing abnormal or untrue could remain in its presence. The abnormal and undesirable will dissolve first.

Sickness falls. Death stops. Tempers and passions flee. These things follow the preaching of truth. Then the visible heavens will roll away like a scroll and the material earth is clean dissolved. Just unadulterated truth will finally effect this.

Do you notice that Nebuzaradan gave the houses and lands of Jerusalem to those who had not had anything at all before? Well, you must be wise enough to notice that the old ideas that have been snubbed in the past are coming to the front as the most powerful ideas to hold. One of these snubbed ideas is the reality of matter. It is going to be one of the richest ideas of the future.

Another snubbed old idea growing into rich favor is, "there is no reality in sickness." Another one is, "we are already at home in God. There is no future."

Kingdoms of matter rise and fall, philosophies stand high and sink into disrepute, the wise old alchemies are held in derision, but that only the good is true shall increase in favor till all is seen as good indeed; that human history never took place shall be the noblest religion; that God and we are one and the same, the only substance Spirit. This is the last trump of Gabriel — ultimate truth.

*March 6, 1892*

# Lesson XI

# SPIRITUAL IDEAS

*Ezekiel 4:9, 36:25-38*

This lesson was written down by Ezekiel as concerning the miracle-working nature of God. He hereby shows what is quite true, viz., that you do not have to deserve great and unexpected blessings before getting them. They are likely to be showered down on heathen-minded people (those who know nothing of spiritual ideas); on carnal-minded people (those who know that there are spiritual teachings, but they like money and food and clothes better); on hard-hearted people (those who care for nothing and nobody), and upon the spiritually-inclined alike.

The law of cause and effect deals with the fruits of thoughts. *"He that createth the fruit of the lips."* The grace and mercy and bounty of God transcend law. You will receive all these anyhow. It is a great rest for the mind to know that it is blessed with some wonderful gifts whether it deserves them or not, and that it is likely to have splendid signs of the good bounty of Jehovah any minute.

Pious people have often regretted this mystery, but they have not been able to stop it. They verily have wished that the sun did not shine quite so brightly on the circus tent as on the camp-meeting, but it did. They have often wished that such gambling and speculating kinds of people did not get all the money and things, but they did. Sometimes quite undesirable kinds of folks have been empowered to do beautiful healing, while the highly moral have been slow at such "works." No matter how exasperating to those who think they ought to be rewarded for being better than their neighbors, it still keeps on.

Ezekiel feels the transcendentally-good God speaking through him in this lesson, as, *"I will call for the corn and I will lay no famine upon you, not for your sakes, but that they shall know that I am the Lord."*

All good things, from shoes to synagogues, from the Gospel to the baby's prattle, are from the Lord.

Such a rest to know you do not have to be good in order to get good things. So the father and mother who refuse the boy his breakfast or dinner or supper or bed because he has been naughty are far, far from God-like.

Such a rest to know that the ravens and robins do not have to pray and praise and have faith in some kind of a god in order to get their breakfast. The good Father feeds and suns and warms them whether they praise and pray or not.

This is what makes God the Lord so beautiful. He asks you to merit nothing. There is a law of cause and effect whereby, if one keeps refusing good, he need not have it by and by, as, for instance, the mind refuses honor, integrity, and the respect of friends, so he need not have them; but these blessings are scattered thickly. He may keep throwing away his money and home until they are gone, but he had them sent to him whether he deserved them or not.

Anybody may expect wonderful miracles of good any moment. One may be so hardened in heart that his neighbors are afraid of him and suddenly have a "heart of flesh" come into him as he tells here.

Just at the moment when he feels hardest the lightning of spirit makes a rift in the mental sphere round him and he sees how good God is (not how angry He is) and suddenly loves Him. Just when the heart is most bitter and despairing a rift is made in the cloud of ideas, and the tenderness and mercy of God (not His hardness and absence) are realized, and love and adoration quicken us. It is no use to try to scare people into being good for the sake of the rewards of goodness. Rewards do not come for being good. The stake, the rack, the jail, public scorn have always been doled out to those who have urged being good for the sake of the rewards of goodness.

Come, let us tell how bountifully indulgent God is — how He is love, whether we love or not; how He feeds, whether we praise or not; how He clothes, whether we pray or not; how He inspires us with genius, whether we have faith in Him or not. The constant description of the goodness and bounty, and mercy and tenderness, and love of God has the most marvelous effect upon the atmosphere. The cold, feeling mind alone in some splendid room, suddenly feels the vibrating mental messages and is moved with compassion. "I love Thee for Thy goodness; forgive me. I will help my brother's children whom I have ignored. Help me to be merciful and kind."

Nobody had need to preach about how that cold, unfeeling mind had stiffened the joints, and show the rigor of cause and effect in order to heal them. They are now healed.

Ezekiel here gives one of those "treatments" to the captive Jews which, if we will read over often, will hasten the loosing of the bonds of captivity for all the earth. All men will feel their minds break open and warm at such mental messages. We might cross out his ideas of remembering our badness and "loathing our sinfulness," for God, you know remembers nothing. *"Their sins will I remember no more against them forever." "They shall forget misery as waters that pass away."*

All those prophets of ancient times were tinged more or less with their past teachings. Shake off everything that you have been taught. Stop remembering anything. It is one of the best practices you can undertake. Forget everything purposely for a few minutes every day. When you come to recollection again what do you suppose you will remember? That which is good. Try it. Try again. Keep it up for years. It is natural for you to remember only just the good. It is artificial to remember the bad. You must be very world-taught if you cherish the past, and so forgetting on purpose may be the only healing practice you need. If you are in trouble and have tried many ways to get out, sit down and forget everything, good, bad and indifferent. The nature of your mind unclothed by ideas is clear with intelligence, bold with understanding, able with right action.

Success and prosperity are your divine nature. The ideas that you are clothed with are very unnecessary. Strip yourself of them at once. Carlyle said that the ideas we are clothed with are "a shadow system gathered round over me."

Ezekiel here holds up a few of his old pieces of his old shell, a few rags of his old teachings, which we will draw our pencil through, for as God never said any such thing we have no time to waste believing that we have to be hunting up how bad we used to be.

There was a man in India four years ago who could cause you to forget everything. He could hold you still in the cleansing solution of forgetfulness till you should touch mind to mind with God. Then suddenly you would spring from this mental "bath" (such as Ezekiel speaks of here), and every bone, muscle, nerve, convolution, would be smiling and dancing with health. Every thought would be entranced with its own beauty and wisdom.

People flocked to him to be healed. One woman spoke to God in such a fashion that she forgot everything except His presence and was cured of dropsy by so doing.

This washing and cleansing that Ezekiel promises we are all to have at last along with Jewry, are simply forgetting everything which the man had such a knack at making people do. Have you ever tried forgetting everything? No. Then it is time you tried it. If you are very busy all day, take the time just as you are about to sleep at night. Think nothing — nothing, on purpose. Sleep will help you. Sleep is an effort on your part to forget. Descartes, the Frenchman, learned to forget when his mind was just loaded with items. So can you.

Of course you will find written in indelible characters the good and so when you first open your eyes in the morning there will be a thought of "something good is coming to me."

If you are awake in the night, practice forgetting. People are always kept awake in the night for their own good. "The Lord holdeth mine eyes waking." Their whole affairs can be managed by night thoughts. By day they are tangled with other people's ideas. By night they are alone with God. God is their friend. "There is a friend that sticketh closer than a brother." Talk with this friend. Tell Him all your needs. Tell Him your plans no matter how bad your purposes are. Tell God with whom you lie awake.

Wisdom and greatness will awake in the morning with you. If you have changed your plans by morning you will still be successful. By this lesson you may know that you never made any mistakes. God was your past.

*"I am Alpha."* By this you may know that you never can make any mistakes. God is your future, *"I am Omega."* By this you may know that nothing can hurt you.

*"My presence shall go with thee."* By this you may not think that it is by any fault of yours at all that you have evils fallen upon you. And it will be no virtue of yours that your blessings come to recognize, "Not for your sakes."

This God who asks nothing and does all is the kind to describe to make the airs warm and the earthquakes cease; the heavens drop down kindness to every creature whether he deserves it or not, and violence to cease forever; the winds to bring you good news from a far country and youth to come again to your wasted heart: home to fold you round and right words to distil as dew from your lips. It is not the deserts of the Jews but their being that is blessed.

It is not your worthiness (praise be to the true God) but the fact of your being that shall cause you to feel this treatment of Ezekiel in its fullness. The planet is being treated to forget. The nations are being treated to forget. So the planet will cease from cyclones and the nations from carnage. "Nature abhors a vacuum." When you forget you are a vacuum, what do you suppose wishes to kiss your divine nature if freed from its memories? All good wishes toward you. What do you suppose will wish to kiss you if you forget the good and forget the good only? Why more bad things, of course, will hasten to greet their own. So it is well to forget everything. At the uncovered center is God. God is good! And thus, *"Lo! My own shall come to me."*

March 13, 1892

## Lesson XII

## ALL FLESH IS GRASS

*Isaiah 40:1-10*

There are four verses in this lesson which contain all the Science of God ever announced to the world. They are the first twelve lessons of the Science, and the second twelve also.

The first set of twelve lessons has already been given very plainly, and is beginning to work its way in the world of sense and intellect. The second set of twelve lessons can come clearly apparent only to those who accept in understanding the first twelve.

If a student finds himself suddenly in possession of the second set of lessons and then goes and tells thereof, he is soon hushed up, and finds himself obliged to go tenderly over the first lessons line upon line and precept upon precept, because his hearers tell him he is annihilating their God, destroying the office and character of Christ, denying the Bible. He must then patiently tell them that God is indestructible, irresistible Substance, Christ is Eternal Truth, the Word of God is infallible.

He does not insist at this point upon telling what he knows to be true, viz., that their God is nowhere, their Christ is a hoax, their Bible an imagination. It must come to each mind by itself that the true God, the true Christ, the true Bible are infinitely incapable of such dealings as the outward wordings of the external Bible proclaim or human observations argue.

The verses that tell the whole story are: *"Speak ye comfortably unto Jerusalem, that her warfare is accomplished, for she hath received of the Lord's hand, double for all her sins" "Make straight in the desert a highway for our God" "All flesh is grass" "The Lord will come with a strong hand, and His arm shall rule for Him."*

Any mind that has ever listened to the voice of God at its center, and has pledged itself to love and believe in God, is Jerusalem. Unto this mind with its body and human lot, it is promised, *"The Lord will take away from thee all sickness, and will put none of the evil diseases of Egypt upon thee"* (Deuteronomy 7:15) *"In famine He shall redeem thee from death, and in war from the power of the sword"* (Job 5:20). *"Bread shall be given him, his wafers shall be sure"* (Isaiah 33:16). *"He will cover thee with His feathers and under His wings shall thou trust"* (Psalms 91:4). *"The Almighty shall be thy defense, and thou shall have plenty of silver"* (Job 22:25) *"Thou shall run and not be weary, walk and not faint"* (Isaiah 40:31). *"He shall give His angels charge over thee to keep thee lest at any time thou dash thy foot against a stone"* (Psalms 91:11).

The Egypt mind gets no such promises. The Egypt mind is the mind that dwells in the senses and has never listened to the voice of the Spirit. It has never pledged itself to live after the dictates of righteousness. Here Jerusalem has been suffering great tribulations in spite of the wonderful promises. How is this?

Because she has entangled her mind with imaginations of ways of getting a living, of learning, of happiness, not in accord with the teachings of the Spirit. Looking at the ways of the world, she has felt that she "must do in Rome as the Romans do." She speaks of God as her rest, and fears accidents. She speaks of God as her health, and looks to material things for her healing. She says; "The merciful man is merciful to his beast," and cuts off the helpless horses' tails to do like the world. Thus is Jerusalem taking at some point of her experience, the fruits of compromise.

But the Truth works also. The Truth the mind tells comes unto its fruitage as well as the error the mind thinks. Then when error has reached its highest point of pain, the truth comes like a healing balm, "Speak comfortably unto Jerusalem."

If in your childhood, some true word kept conning itself over in your mind, it will come to you at your sorest need as a healing. This is what is meant by "Man's extremity is God's opportunity." But it is the mind pledged to faith in such Truth that gets the healing by its own words, not the mind living in its imaginations. The affairs of your life are met at their direst extremities by certain words you once spoke, just as your bodily health is overtaken. I hope you believed this passage at some period of your life; *"Call thou upon Me in the day of adversity, and I will deliver thee"* (Jeremiah 39:17). *"It will come with unexpected successes at some least probable moment, in such an hour as ye think not"* (Matthew 24:44).

Why not? Make straight through that desert of non-expectation for the fulfillment of each one of them. *"The desert shall blossom as the rose." "I will satisfy thy soul in drought."* The most marvelous things you can think of are the things to expect in the Science of God. In a certain city where the rich have everything and the poor have nothing, there has arisen a meek sect of people who say they can call upon the Father-Mother God for everything, even to money. They do not seem to have any visible means of getting their living, yet they are honorable in their dealings and never run into debt. The people of that city have stoned them, thrown mud at them and broken their windows, though they are harmless and unretaliating.

Would not you rather know how to call upon God, in whose hands are all the treasures of the hills, than to know how to make a deal on the

Board of Trade that would cost every starving child one penny more for his supper, which penny he cannot get? Why do they not stone those who gather the productions of the generous earth into corners and make it so hard for the poor, instead of those who are making a path through the desert of hard times for the marvelous God to walk through? Would not you rather know the process by which the noble Ram Lai called down the white fog on the hills of Keitung to defend his friend from the would-be murderers, than to know the latest device in electric alarms for burglars? There on the hills of desolation in the desert mound of no prospect for help, was the marvelous God of defense.

Would not you rather know the mystic language by which the three wise men met on the plains of no fruitage under the white stars of midnight, never having met before, coming by sure steps, unsought by cablegrams, telegrams, letters, to find in each other friendship unfailing, comradeship in all things, than to know how our ministers to England or France, or our fair women delegates are received at foreign courts? There on the sands, with only the moon for a light, the marvelous God taught His friendship for man.

Come — desert spot in the heart where you do not expect love, do not expect home, do not expect fulfillment — awake! The God of the nations commandeth, expect! This is the hour when the desert must bloom. *"Is anything too hard for Me, saith our God"* (Genesis 18:14). Let them keep their gold. God will provide. Let them corner our bread and meat. God will provide. Let them preach death and sorrow. God will bring to life, and comfort them that mourn.

All the riches of earth shall be no more counted in that day when the desert lifts up her head than the air is now measured out. We do not hold our breath lest the air fail us. Here on the desert we hold fast no riches. God will provide. Do you rise into faith as this simple text opens its loving meaning to you?

*"Here on the lap of our mother we rest;*

*God is our home.*

*Here none shall pursue us,*

*Here none can undo us.*

*We walk with the blest.*

*God is our home."*

The next text is *"All flesh is grass."* That is the second lesson of Science, the second lesson of the first course. Here we count it as true that all earthly things are symbols only. Thought is the substance. Then we push the meaning still further and say that the thoughts that show forth in material things are as *non est as* the material things themselves.

Is that too metaphysical for you? Oh no, it is not. You already believe that God, the Mind of the universe, fills all space and place and where, *"Am not I God? Do I not fill heaven and earth? Is there any besides Me? Nay, I know-not any"* (Jeremiah 23:24). Then there is but one Mind thinking thoughts. So the thoughts that produce material things with their clashings and sorrows are no thoughts at all. It has a very uplifting effect upon the mind and a very enchanting power over your affairs to understand this text. Down through the walls steps the transcendent Jesus into your presence. The granules of matter offer no resistance to the Mind that knows them not. Spirit will bear witness with Spirit that there is only one substance at all, and that is your soul. *"The flesh profiteth nothing,"* speaks the entrancing Friend as He lifts you out of the memory of the past — out of the pain of the present.

*"Alone with Thee my soul walks fearless.*

*Mantled by Thee I rest in happy peace;*

*Standing 'mid scenes I once mourned as cheerless,*

*I now joyous smile, proclaiming swift release."*

The fourth text takes us by one touch of inspiration to the unspoken top of the Mount of Paradise, where in the workshop of Jehovah we watch the Christian doctrine redeem the race.

*"The Lord God shall come with a strong hand and His arm shall rule for Him."* This is prophecy. John the Revelator saw the same moment and on the friendless isle of Patmos, rejoiced in our day. In the great pyramid of Gizeh, the north star looked down the mystic shaft of ages ago and

wrote across her golden breast that the line where it is intended history shall end and prophecy be fulfilled, is today. John spoke it by a figure. He saw the holy Science as a woman. Take your mind away from men and women and think only of the Holy Spirit as you read how he saw the woman clothed as the sun, having on her head the crown of twelve stars, and the moon under her feet. This is the Science of God, and it gives to the world the Man-Child who shall rule all nations with a rod of iron. The Man-Child of Science is the strong teaching of Science, the strong and invincible idea that springs forth at its highest point of instruction, viz, that man is God and God is man.

The Spirit of man and the Spirit of God may say, *"I am that I am." "There is a Spirit in man, and the inspiration of the Almighty giveth him understanding"*(Job 32:8). Who told them to change the royal arch word of God ever speaking in the soul, "I am that I am," in Masonry to "I was, but am no more?"

Am not I *"Alpha and Omega, the beginning and the end?"* (Revelations 1:8). Who said that the flesh might speak? Shall any have voice save God? The "strong right hand" of this text means the efficient thought, or strong idea of God. The idea of mind is the son, or man-child. The idea that the "I am that I am" in man is the "I am that I am" of God shall rule all nations with a rod of iron, though the Science that gave it birth may have to be driven into the wilderness of the scorn of the world.

Now think of all those who teach the Science, as the Science itself, and with the twelfth of Revelation, follow their experience after they give forth their noblest conclusion. The chased black in the everglades was no more at bay than they, as the very abstraction of evil hurries them into poverty, pain, tribulation. At this point, they are met with the strange information that holding the name Jesus Christ in mind forces all the issues between Good and evil into their own experience.

If Jesus Christ *"had not where to lay His head,"* neither shall they. If He was *"despised and rejected,"* so shall they be — by holding His name in mind. But "the earth helped the woman." The very wilderness shall yield you the corn, and the wine of dominion over all the ways of the flesh. "His own arm shall get Him rule." Throw your highest truth into the arena, and let it fight for itself. Jesus Christ teaches you dominion. It is Jesus Christ in you that is the "I am that I am."

*"He shall rule from sea to sea, and from the river to the uttermost parts of the earth."*
*(Zechariah 9:10)*

John, speaking in a figure, saw the holy Science fly away with the "wings of a great eagle." The two wings with which you who enter into the Science may fly, are two words — "within and without." God is both within you and without you, the here and the there, the beginning and the end.

To you forever the breath comes, *"I am satisfied in Thee"* and from you forever the response must go back, *"I am satisfied in thee."* From your breath in the wilderness of earthly seemings, the triumphant response, *"I am satisfied in Thee."* From the heart-fires of the earth, from the crawling things and the stones comes the nourishing message, *"I am satisfied in Thee."* And from your wise heart, no timid answer steals; like a radiant light your word lets fall, *"I am satisfied in Thee."*

Thus they that know the Science are "nourished." Its arm gets them rule. *"Thus shall thou be in league with the stones of the field, and the beasts of the field shall be at peace with thee."* (Job 5:23).

*March 20, 1892*

# Lesson XIII

## THE OLD AND THE NEW CONTRASTED

*REVIEW*

Every three months we have a review of the past twelve weeks' lessons. This is the review.

History is good. Bacon says, "History makes men wise."If so, we will study history. Therefore get wisdom."

History is not memorized dates of battles, names of kings, lengths of dynasties. History is noting from the regular results of causes that, "Things equal to the same thing are equal to each other."

History is prophecy, at its highest mission. We have been told that astronomy is the only science that has reached the third stage of science, viz., prophecy.

The boy at his "Horace" is told that he must not inquire what will happen tomorrow — *"Quid sit futurum eras, fuge quaerere."* ("How is the future to be, do not look for it.") In the *Inferno* of Dante, those who tell the future are placed in the fourth ditch with their faces turned backward, so as to have no hopes but to see everything as passed.

It has always seemed lawful for mankind to pay historians for the privilege of listening to their memorizing of past events, but totally illegitimate to reflect that the laborer in the fields of future history is equally worthy of his hire. *"The laborer is worthy of his hire"* (Luke 10:7).

Paul sees that to know the future from the past, to see all future as now, is a great science, therefore he says, *"Despise not prophesying"* (I Thessalonians 5:20). And among the gifts of the Holy Spirit he mentions prophesying as quite equal to preaching in the pulpit, or healing by prayers. Being all the evidence of the Holy Spirit, he speaks as reverently of one as of the other. He likes to have students in the Science of Life as intelligent as those in the science of numbers. The mathematician will always be sure that to extract the square root of the sum of the squares of the perpendicular and base will give him the hypotenuse of a triangle. The student of Life Science may always be sure that *"envy is rottenness of the bones"* (Proverbs 14:30); *"pride goeth before destruction, and an haughty spirit before a fall."* (Proverbs 18:18); *"the hypocrite's hope shall perish"* (Job 3:13).

So when Paul sees a man envious he must say, "Your bones will fail you." When he sees a woman smiling and smiling and smiling while her heart is breaking, he must say, "You will be often disappointed in your hopes, because the without and the within must be exactly alike, for only so is harmony."

He must say that the form of hypocrisy where the lips tell of faith in God while the heart hates God, will bring different kinds of disappointments from those where the face smiles so that no one else may be hurt while the heart is hurt. He knows that very proud people will come to destruction along that line where their pride lies. He knows that scornful feelings against others will bring accidents into the family. He also knows that there are certain words which taken into mind will antidote all these things. He cannot help seeing that from the very nature of the case you must have a peculiar future laid out for you and that therefore you need peculiar treatment to antidote or advantage it.

The history of the last twelve lessons being measured against our future lessons, we will find we have certain conclusions with which to proceed. First, we find that the less prejudice we have in mind, for or against anyone or anything, the clearer sighted we shall be.

Second, we find that knowing this causes so much prejudice to drop from the mentality of so many people that very soon millions of people will be able to tell exactly what is true in all the old religions.

Third, we find that the prophets and kings mentioned in the history we have been studying, each thought the others more obligated to deal with God for support, defense, health, life, etc., than themselves, which brought sorrowful defeat. By this we learn to cling with strong joy to the text, *"With God is no respect of persons"* (2 Chron. 19-7; Romans 2:11; Ephesians 6:9; Col. 3:25) and make sure that a prophet is no nearer God than a king, while a sewing-girl can do as much feeding of the poor, as a billionaire.

Fourth, we discover that what a Draconis looking down through the shaft of the Gizeh pyramid read for this age is fulfilled, viz., that now at this period, history closes, prophecies are fulfilled, the golden age begins.

Under the gleaming candle of the first idea, we discover that the ancient religionist missed the sight of his own powers when he said that if the lower classes should be told that there were rules of thought that would identify man with God, they must have hot wax or boiling oil poured into their ears.

That notion was a black square held before their eyes and a stopper for their ears which nothing but giving it up would remove. They had the very order in which Spiritual Science arranges the descriptions of mental unfoldment. They told what certain words would do and they had the identical ideas of Jesus Christ. They said that "it is by the divine word that the sick are most surely healed." They had a rule for spiritualization of mind, which, if they had dropped that odd idea that God made great distinction between men and women, high and low, etc., would have worked so as to sweep physical misery off the planet.

Perhaps you would like to see how very close (excluding the physical exercises) this rule was to ours. This is the idea, not the language: keep perfectly still, not even breathing, repeating twelve times the word, "Om," (this is our Omnipresence, Omnipotence, Omniscience.) You must be knowing all this time there is no presence around you or within you except God. Then draw in the breath and hold it while repeating the same word, "Om," 24 times. Do this without fear and -without idleness for three months. In the fourth month you will feel the Spirit. (Our fourth idea of reason is faith or confidence in the presence of the Spirit so strong that we feel it.) In the fifth month, you will feel the Spirit moving through you. (Our fifth idea of Science is that, "God works through us to will and to do.") In the sixth month, you will become God. (Our sixth statement of reason is that we are one with God through understanding God.)

Keshub Chunder Sen, the head of the Brahma Somaj, told some Englishmen that it was their prejudices that kept them performing physically to bring about that which mind could accomplish. He caused some Englishmen to see what was then going on in a distant part of the city by annihilating space for a moment in their minds.

There are wonderful things of Spirit for those who do not cling to their former teachers. Just think of finding that it is true, practically, that what Dante saw and must acknowledge from neo-Platonism and agnosticism will work a lofty state of mind full of power and wisdom, viz., "God is exalted above virtue and knowledge, and above good and evil." This statement will swing you out of the reach of the need of books. You transcend them. You know them without studying them. Out of the reach of human failures and foibles — you transcend them. The mind is like what it thinks, and it externalizes what it is like.

By the third lesson of our study of Hebrew history, we note that Isaiah, Jeremiah, Ezekial, all stood helpless spectators of destruction because they thought the kings ought to stop the destructions. Should God invest a king with more executive ability than a prophet? No. The mere fact of their seeing that safety was possible, was evidence that they were the ones to defend the cities. It is no use to know that your envy is spoiling your bones if there is no way to cure you of envy. No use to name evil if you cannot stop it.

There is only one power that can defend cities, cure envies, stop crimes. That is the power that leads captivity itself captive — that is the mind trained to be one with Christ. Any mind has the power to lead captivity itself captive, if envy makes rottenness of bones, cure the envy and the bones are all right. The plow-boy can cure the envy of the king. If thirst after righteousness unsatisfied makes drunkenness, the right thoughts being given, drunkenness will be cured. The streetcar conductor may give the right thoughts. If prayers will support your family, defend your city, the shoemaker may demonstrate support in time of famine and keep the tidal-wave, cyclone, earthquake from destroying your city.

There is no such thing as helplessness. It is all a mistake. We can bring to pass that which we see ought to be brought to pass. If we have been taught less than this, we are mistaken. When Isaiah saw that judging not after the senses would work miracles, he ought to have judged not after the senses.

A certain printer, who knew very few books, heard that certain words would have the effect of healing, so he spoke within his mind those words and actually he could not see sickness in people and could not hear people tell of their ailments for several days. During that time, he healed deformities and infirmities of the worst kind. Isaiah also saw that it was the duty of the people to deny that they inherited anything at all from their forefathers.

By a little skillful judgment, you will trace how you can get clear of poverty and pain by lopping that belief in heredity off your mind. Many people need to lift the yoke of generations off their necks.

You remember that the people that opposed Jesus said that His blood should descend upon us. So we have to say: "I refuse the consequences of your foolishness and ignorance." Speak straight to the whole line of ancestors back of you. Jesus Christ said: *"Call no man upon earth your father, for One is your Father, even God"* (Matthew 23:9).

When these prophets said that there should be nothing to hurt or kill, for a man's word was his only burden, they taught us to particularize what they theorized. We will take none of those words they laid upon their already overburdened shoulders. We will not be burdened, or drowned, or martyred as they were. They taught us better. If Isaiah's words walked him straight to a hollow carob tree to be sawn asunder, let us keep clear of his words. If Jeremiah's words led him straight to a martyr's fate in Egypt, let us fight shy of his words. If Ezekiel's words led him straight to be murdered in Bagdad, let us not use his words. What made them tell that nothing should hurt and then describe hurts? Why mourn over sins if they are all delusions? Each true idea is sweet wine. Confidence in the idea is strength like iron. The hatreds of mankind are a strychnine quality tingling the airs around those who speak Truth.

You know that strychnine, wine, and iron make a wonderful tonic in the realm of materiality. Suppose Ruskin, with his spiritual ideas, had had confidence in their defensive powers, and when thousands sent the poisons of their hates at him he had said, "You are good for me," to all that came, instead of flinching at criticisms so that his brain spoiled. He would have taken a new lease on intelligence. A new strength would have invigorated him.

In the science of mind, we are called to note that one after another of earth's great characters reaches the summit of his originality, and from that moment, "threshes of straw" — that is, keeps harping on what he has been teaching instead of rising from the turning point of his career with new splendor. After the child turns to be a youth, he must not play with his childish playthings; if he does, he is idiotic. After the splendor of the great man's intellect has reached its summit, if he returns to the same thoughts again, what? Senility.

You know how we have to be always telling what such men and women "used to do." Wherefore thus? Somewhere they refused to go on. They should have rested a moment like a lion on his haunches, and then fearless of all things, sprung to the golden age of the new doctrine offered them. All things that are true of Spirit are true of man here and now. The senses reach their limit in power to please. The intellect ceases to be satisfied with its highest learnings. Now what?

Oh, you do not need to return to your learnings, your theories, your former teachings. Your new powers, much more splendid than the hey-day of manhood, may now spring. Here is the time to listen to the higher call. Rest till the new age teaches you how to transcend yourself. There is a call higher than intellect. Let it lead. "Lead Thou me on." There are powers the combined energies of physics and intellect cannot touch. Listen now to the Spirit. You must not notice the teachings of men.

As the first statements of Science reject the evidences of the senses, so the last statements of Science reject the conclusions of the intellect — nay, reject the intellect itself. The intellect has no intelligence. Spirit is the only intelligence. And here whoever refuses, marks his face with the first wrinkle of age and frosts his hair with the first breath of senility.

Do you say these things are an honor? Oh, no. God is immortal. Intelligence, immortal renewal. Feebleness and death are not God-like, "Be ye holy (whole) as I am holy." The highest spiritual doctrine for life here and now — not for beyond the grave.

*March 27, 1892*

.

# Notes

## Other Books by Emma Curtis Hopkins

- *Class Lessons of 1888 (WiseWoman Press)*
- *Bible Interpretations (WiseWoman Press)*
- *Esoteric Philosophy in Spiritual Science (WiseWoman Press)*
- *Genesis Series*
- *High Mysticism (WiseWoman Press)*
- *Self Treatments with Radiant I Am (WiseWoman Press)*
- *Gospel Series (WiseWoman Press)*
- *Judgment Series in Spiritual Science (WiseWoman Press)*
- *Drops of Gold (WiseWoman Press)*
- *Resume (WiseWoman Press)*
- *Scientific Christian Mental Practice (DeVorss)*

## Books about Emma Curtis Hopkins and her teachings

- *Emma Curtis Hopkins, Forgotten Founder of New Thought* – Gail Harley
- *Unveiling Your Hidden Power: Emma Curtis Hopkins' Metaphysics for the 21st Century* (also as a Workbook and as A Guide for Teachers) – Ruth L. Miller
- *Power to Heal: Easy reading biography for all ages* –Ruth Miller

To find more of Emma's work, including some previously unpublished material, log on to:

www.emmacurtishopkins.com

# WISEWOMAN PRESS

1521 NE Jantzen Ave #143
Portland, Oregon 97217
800.603.3005
www.wisewomanpress.com

### *Books Published by WiseWoman Press*

## By Emma Curtis Hopkins

- *Resume*
- *Gospel Series*
- *Class Lessons of 1888*
- *Self Treatments including Radiant I Am*
- *High Mysticism*
- *Esoteric Philosophy in Spiritual Science*
- *Drops of Gold Journal*
- *Judgment Series*
- *Bible Interpretations: series I, II and III*

## By Ruth L. Miller

- *Unveiling Your Hidden Power: Emma Curtis Hopkins' Metaphysics for the 21st Century*
- *Coming into Freedom: Emily Cady's Lessons in Truth for the 21st Century*
- *150 Years of Healing: The Founders and Science of New Thought*
- *Power Beyond Magic: Ernest Holmes Biography*
- *Power to Heal: Emma Curtis Hopkins Biography*
- *The Power of Unity: Charles Fillmore Biography*
- *Uncommon Prayer*
- *Spiritual Success*
- *Finding the Path*

**Watch our website for release dates and order information! - www.wisewomanpress.com**

# List of Bible Interpretation Series with date from 1st to 14th Series.

This list is complete through the fourteenth Series. Emma produced at least thirty Series of Bible Interpretations.

She followed the Bible Passages provided by the International Committee of Clerics who produced the Bible Quotations for each year's use in churches all over the world.

Emma used these for her column of Bible Interpretations in both the Christian Science Magazine, at her Seminary and in the Chicago Inter-Ocean Newspaper.

# First Series

## July 5 - September 27, 1891

| | | |
|---|---|---|
| Lesson 1 | The Word Made Flesh<br>*John 1:1-18* | July 5th |
| Lesson 2 | Christ's First Disciples<br>John 1:29-42 | July 12th |
| Lesson 3 | All Is Divine Order<br>*John 2:1-11* (Christ's first Miracle) | July 19th |
| Lesson 4 | Jesus Christ and Nicodemus<br>*John 3:1-17* | July 26th |
| Lesson 5 | Christ at Samaria<br>*John 4:5-26* (Christ at Jacob's Well) | August 2nd |
| Lesson 6 | Self-condemnation<br>*John 5:17-30* (Christ's Authority) | August 9th |
| Lesson 7 | Feeding the Starving<br>*John 6:1-14* (The Five Thousand Fed) | August 16th |
| Lesson 8 | The Bread of Life<br>*John 6:26-40* (Christ the Bread of Life) | August 23rd |
| Lesson 9 | The Chief Thought<br>*John 7:31-34* (Christ at the Feast) | August 30th |
| Lesson 10 | Continue the Work<br>*John 8:31-47* | September 6th |
| Lesson 11 | Inheritance of Sin<br>*John 9:1-11, 35-38* (Christ and the Blind Man) | September 13th |
| Lesson 12 | The Real Kingdom<br>*John 10:1-16* (Christ the Good Shepherd) | September 20th |
| Lesson 13 | In Retrospection | September 27th<br>Review |

## Second Series

### October 4 - December 27, 1891

| | | |
|---|---|---|
| Lesson 1 | Mary and Martha<br>*John 11:21-44* | October 4th |
| Lesson 2 | Glory of Christ<br>*John 12:20-36* | October 11th |
| Lesson 3 | Good in Sacrifice<br>*John 13:1-17* | October 18th |
| Lesson 4 | Power of the Mind<br>*John 14:13; 15-27* | October 25th |
| Lesson 5 | Vines and Branches<br>*John 15:1-16* | November 1st |
| Lesson 6 | Your Idea of God<br>*John 16:1-15* | November 8th |
| Lesson 7 | Magic of His Name<br>*John 17:1-19* | November 15th |
| Lesson 8 | Jesus and Judas<br>*John 18:1-13* | November 22nd |
| Lesson 9 | Scourge of Tongues<br>*John 19:1-16* | November 29th |
| Lesson 10 | Simplicity of Faith<br>*John 19:17-30* | December 6th |
| Lesson 11 | Christ is All in All<br>*John 20: 1-18* | December 13th |
| Lesson 12 | Risen With Christ<br>*John 21:1-14* | December 20th |
| Lesson 13 | The Spirit is Able<br>Review of Year | December 27th |

# *Third Series*

## January 3 - March 27, 1892

| | | |
|---|---|---|
| Lesson 1 | A Golden Promise<br>*Isaiah 11:1-10* | January 3rd |
| Lesson 2 | The Twelve Gates<br>*Isaiah 26:1-10* | January 10th |
| Lesson 3 | Who Are Drunkards<br>*Isaiah 28:1-13* | January 17th |
| Lesson 4 | Awake Thou That Sleepest<br>*Isaiah 37:1-21* | January 24th |
| Lesson 5 | The Healing Light<br>*Isaiah 53:1-21* | January 31st |
| Lesson 6 | True Ideal of God<br>*Isaiah 55:1-13* | February 7th |
| Lesson 7 | Heaven Around Us<br>*Jeremiah 31 14-37* | February 14th |
| Lesson 8 | But One Substance<br>*Jeremiah 36:19-31* | February 21st |
| Lesson 9 | Justice of Jehovah<br>*Jeremiah 37:11-21* | February 28th |
| Lesson 10 | God and Man Are One<br>*Jeremiah 39:1-10* | March 6th |
| Lesson 11 | Spiritual Ideas<br>*Ezekiel 4:9, 36:25-38* | March 13th |
| Lesson 12 | All Flesh is Grass<br>*Isaiah 40:1-10* | March 20th |
| Lesson 13 | The Old and New Contrasted<br>Review | March 27th |

## Fourth Series

### April 3 - June 26, 1892

| | | |
|---|---|---|
| Lesson 1 | Realm of Thought<br>*Psalm 1:1-6* | April 3rd |
| Lesson 2 | The Power of Faith<br>*Psalm 2:1-12* | April 10th |
| Lesson 3 | Let the Spirit Work<br>*Psalm 19:1-14* | April 17th |
| Lesson 4 | Christ is Dominion<br>*Psalm 23:1-6* | April 24th |
| Lesson 5 | External or Mystic<br>*Psalm 51:1-13* | May 1st |
| Lesson 6 | Value of Early Beliefs<br>*Psalm 72: 1-9* | May 8th |
| Lesson 7 | Truth Makes Free<br>*Psalm 84:1-12* | May 15th |
| Lesson 8 | False Ideas of God<br>*Psalm 103:1-22* | May 22nd |
| Lesson 9 | But Men Must Work<br>*Daniel 1:8-21* | May 29th |
| Lesson 10 | Artificial Helps<br>*Daniel 2:36-49* | June 5th |
| Lesson 11 | Dwelling in Perfect Life<br>*Daniel 3:13-25* | June 12th |
| Lesson 12 | Which Streak Shall Rule<br>*Daniel 6:16-28* | June 19th |
| Lesson 13 | See Things as They Are<br>Review of 12 Lessons | June 26th |

# Fifth Series

## July 3 - September 18, 1892

| | | |
|---|---|---|
| Lesson 1 | The Measure of a Master<br>*Acts 1:1-12* | July 3rd |
| Lesson 2 | Chief Ideas Rule People<br>*Acts 2:1-12* | July 10th |
| Lesson 3 | New Ideas About Healing<br>*Acts 2:37-47* | July 17th |
| Lesson 4 | Heaven a State of Mind<br>*Acts 3:1-16* | July 24th |
| Lesson 5 | About Mesmeric Powers<br>*Acts 4:1-18* | July 31st |
| Lesson 6 | Points in the Mosaic Law<br>*Acts 4:19-31* | August 7th |
| Lesson 7 | Napoleon's Ambition<br>*Acts 5:1-11* | August 14th |
| Lesson 8 | A River Within the Heart<br>*Acts 5:25-41* | August 21st |
| Lesson 9 | The Answering of Prayer<br>Acts 7: 54-60 - Acts 8: 1-4 | August 28th |
| Lesson 10 | Words Spoken by the Mind<br>*Acts 8:5-35* | September 4th |
| Lesson 11 | Just What It Teaches Us<br>*Acts 8:26-40* | September 11th |
| Lesson 12 | The Healing Principle<br>Review | September 18th |

# Sixth Series

## September 25 - December 18, 1892

| | | |
|---|---|---|
| Lesson 1 | The Science of Christ<br>*1 Corinthians 11:23-34* | September 25th |
| Lesson 2 | On the Healing of Saul<br>*Acts 9:1-31* | October 2nd |
| Lesson 3 | The Power of the Mind Explained<br>*Acts 9:32-43* | October 9th |
| Lesson 4 | Faith in Good to Come<br>*Acts 10:1-20* | October 16th |
| Lesson 5 | Emerson's Great Task<br>*Acts 10:30-48* | October 23rd |
| Lesson 6 | The Teaching of Freedom<br>*Acts 11:19-30* | October 30th |
| Lesson 7 | Seek and Ye Shall Find<br>*Acts 12:1-17* | November 6th |
| Lesson 8 | The Ministry of the Holy Mother<br>*Acts 13:1-13* | November 13th |
| Lesson 9 | The Power of Lofty Ideas<br>*Acts 13:26-43* | November 20th |
| Lesson 10 | Sure Recipe for Old Age<br>*Acts 13:44-52, 14:1-7* | November 27th |
| Lesson 11 | The Healing Principle<br>*Acts 14:8-22* | December 4th |
| Lesson 12 | Washington's Vision<br>*Acts 15:12-29* | December 11th |
| Lesson 13 | Review of the Quarter | December 18th |
| Partial Lesson | Shepherds and the Star | December 25th |

# Seventh Series

## January 1 - March 31, 1893

| | | |
|---|---|---|
| Lesson 1 | All is as Allah Wills | January 1st |
| | *Ezra 1* | |
| | Khaled Knew that he was of The Genii | |
| | The Coming of Jesus | |
| Lesson 2 | Zerubbabel's High Ideal | January 8th |
| | *Ezra 2:8-13* | |
| | Fulfillments of Prophecies | |
| | Followers of the Light | |
| | Doctrine of Spinoza | |
| Lesson 3 | Divine Rays Of Power | January 15th |
| | *Ezra 4* | |
| | The Twelve Lessons of Science | |
| Lesson 4 | Visions Of Zechariah | January 22nd |
| | *Zechariah 3* | |
| | Subconscious Belief in Evil | |
| | Jewish Ideas of Deity | |
| | Fruits of Mistakes | |
| Lesson 5 | Aristotle's Metaphysician | January 27th |
| | Missing (See Review for summary) | |
| Lesson 6 | The Building of the Temple | February 3rd |
| | Missing (See Review for summary) | |
| Lesson 7 | Pericles and his Work in building the Temple | |
| | *Nehemiah 13* | February 12th |
| | Supreme Goodness | |
| | On and Upward | |
| Lesson 8 | Ancient Religions | February 19th |
| | *Nehemiah 1* | |
| | The Chinese | |
| | The Holy Spirit | |
| Lesson 9 | Understanding is Strength Part 1 | February 26th |
| | *Nehemiah 13* | |
| Lesson 10 | Understanding is Strength Part 2 | March 3rd |
| | *Nehemiah 13* | |
| Lesson 11 | Way of the Spirit | March 10th |
| | *Esther* | |
| Lesson 12 | Speaking of Right Things | March 17th |
| | *Proverbs 23:15-23* | |
| Lesson 13 | Review | March 24th |

# Eighth Series

## April 2 - June 25, 1893

| | | |
|---|---|---|
| Lesson 1 | The Resurrection | April 2nd |
| | *Matthew 28:1-10* | |
| | One Indestructible | |
| | Life In Eternal Abundance | |
| | The Resurrection | |
| | Shakes Nature Herself | |
| | Gospel to the Poor | |
| Lesson 2 | Universal Energy | April 9th |
| | *Book of Job, Part 1* | |
| Lesson 3 | Strength From Confidence | April 16th |
| | *Book of Job, Part II* | |
| Lesson 4 | The New Doctrine Brought Out | April 23rd |
| | *Book of Job, Part III* | |
| Lesson 5 | The Golden Text | April 30th |
| | *Proverbs 1:20-23* | |
| | Personification Of Wisdom | |
| | Wisdom Never Hurts | |
| | The "Two" Theory | |
| | All is Spirit | |
| Lesson 6 | The Law of Understanding | May 7th |
| | *Proverbs 3* | |
| | Shadows of Ideas | |
| | The Sixth Proposition | |
| | What Wisdom Promises | |
| | Clutch On Material Things | |
| | The Tree of Life | |
| | Prolonging Illuminated Moments | |
| Lesson 7 | Self-Esteem | May 14th |
| | *Proverbs 12:1-15* | |
| | Solomon on Self-Esteem | |
| | The Magnetism of Passing Events | |
| | Nothing Established by Wickedness | |
| | Strength of a Vitalized Mind | |
| | Concerning the "Perverse Heart" | |

| | | |
|---|---|---|
| Lesson 8 | Physical vs. Spiritual Power | May 21st |
| | *Proverbs 23:29-35* | |
| | Law of Life to Elevate the Good and Banish the Bad | |
| | Lesson Against Intemperance | |
| | Good Must Increase | |
| | To Know Goodness Is Life | |
| | The Angel of God's Presence | |
| Lesson 9 | Lesson missing | May 28th |
| | (See Review for concept) | |
| Lesson 10 | Recognizing Our Spiritual Nature | June 4th |
| | *Proverbs 31:10-31* | |
| | Was Called Emanuel | |
| | The covenant of Peace | |
| | The Ways of the Divine | |
| | Union With the Divine | |
| | Miracles Will Be Wrought | |
| Lesson 11 | Intuition | June 11th |
| | *Ezekiel 8:2-3* | |
| | *Ezekiel 9:3-6, 11* | |
| | Interpretation of the Prophet | |
| | Ezekiel's Vision | |
| | Dreams and Their Cause | |
| | Israel and Judah | |
| | Intuition the Head | |
| | Our Limited Perspective | |
| Lesson 12 | The Book of Malachi | June 18th |
| | *Malachi* | |
| | The Power of Faith | |
| | The Exercise of thankfulness | |
| | Her Faith Self-Sufficient | |
| | Burned with the Fires of Truth | |
| | What is Reality | |
| | One Open Road | |
| Lesson 13 | Review of the Quarter | June 25th |
| | *Proverbs 31:10-31* | |

# Ninth Series

## July 2 - September 27, 1893

| | | |
|---|---|---|
| Lesson 1 | Secret of all Power | July 2nd |
| Acts 16: 6-15 | The Ancient Chinese Doctrine of Taoism | |
| | Manifesting of God Powers | |
| | Paul, Timothy, and Silas | |
| | Is Fulfilling as Prophecy | |
| | The Inner Prompting. | |
| | Good Taoist Never Depressed | |
| Lesson 2 | The Flame of Spiritual Verity | July 9th |
| Acts 16:18 | Cause of Contention | |
| | Delusive Doctrines | |
| | Paul's History | |
| | Keynotes | |
| | Doctrine Not New | |
| Lesson 3 | Healing Energy Gifts | July 16th |
| Acts 18:19-21 | How Paul Healed | |
| | To Work Miracles | |
| | Paul Worked in Fear | |
| | Shakespeare's Idea of Loss | |
| | Endurance the Sign of Power | |
| Lesson 4 | Be Still My Soul | July 23rd |
| Acts 17:16-24 | Seeing Is Believing | |
| | Paul Stood Alone | |
| | Lessons for the Athenians | |
| | All Under His Power | |
| | Freedom of Spirit | |
| Lesson 5 | (Missing) Acts 18:1-11 | July 30th |
| Lesson 6 | Missing No Lesson * | August 6th |
| Lesson 7 | The Comforter is the Holy Ghost | August 13th |
| Acts 20 | Requisite for an Orator | |
| | What is a Myth | |
| | Two Important Points | |
| | Truth of the Gospel | |
| | Kingdom of the Spirit | |
| | Do Not Believe in Weakness | |

| | | |
|---|---|---|
| Lesson 8 | Conscious of a Lofty Purpose | August 20th |
| Acts 21 | As a Son of God | |
| | Wherein Paul failed | |
| | Must Give Up the Idea | |
| | Associated with Publicans | |
| | Rights of the Spirit | |
| Lesson 9 | Measure of Understanding | August 27th |
| Acts 24:19-32 | Lesser of Two Evils | |
| | A Conciliating Spirit | |
| | A Dream of Uplifting | |
| | The Highest Endeavor | |
| | Paul at Caesarea | |
| | Preparatory Symbols | |
| | Evidence of Christianity | |
| Lesson 10 | The Angels of Paul | September 3rd |
| Acts 23:25-26 | Paul's Source of Inspiration | |
| | Should Not Be Miserable | |
| | Better to Prevent than Cure | |
| | Mysteries of Providence | |
| Lesson 11 | The Hope of Israel | September 10th |
| Acts 28:20-31 | Immunity for Disciples | |
| | Hiding Inferiorities | |
| | Pure Principle | |
| Lesson 12 | Joy in the Holy Ghost | September 17th |
| Romans 14 | Temperance | |
| | The Ideal Doctrine | |
| | Tells a Different Story | |
| | Hospitals as Evidence | |
| | Should Trust in the Savior | |
| Lesson 13 | Review | September 24th |
| Acts 26-19-32 | The Leveling Doctrine | |
| | Boldness of Command | |
| | Secret of Inheritance | |
| | Power in a Name | |

## Tenth Series

October 1 – December 24, 1893

| | | |
|---|---|---|
| Lesson 1 | *Romans 1:1-19* | October 1st |
| | When the Truth is Known | |
| | Faith in God | |
| | The Faithful Man is Strong | |
| | Glory of the Pure Motive | |
| Lesson 2 | *Romans 3:19-26* | October 8th |
| | Free Grace. | |
| | On the Gloomy Side | |
| | Daniel and Elisha | |
| | Power from Obedience | |
| | Fidelity to His Name | |
| | He Is God | |
| Lesson 3 | *Romans 5* | October 15th |
| | The Healing Principle | |
| | Knows No Defeat. | |
| | In Glorified Realms | |
| | He Will Come | |
| Lesson 4 | *Romans 12:1* | October 22nd |
| | Would Become Free | |
| | Man's Co-operation | |
| | Be Not Overcome | |
| | Sacrifice No Burden | |
| | Knows the Future | |
| Lesson 5 | *I Corinthians 8:1-13* | October 29th |
| | The Estate of Man | |
| | Nothing In Self | |
| | What Paul Believed | |
| | Doctrine of Kurozumi | |
| Lesson 6 | *I Corinthians 12:1-26* | November 5th |
| | Science of The Christ Principle | |
| | Dead from the Beginning | |
| | St. Paul's Great Mission | |
| | What The Spark Becomes | |
| | Chris, All There Is of Man | |
| | Divinity Manifest in Man | |
| | Christ Principle Omnipotent | |

| | | |
|---|---|---|
| Lesson 7 | *II Corinthians 8:1-12*<br>Which Shall It Be?<br>The Spirit is Sufficient<br>Working of the Holy Ghost | November 12th |
| Lesson 8 | *Ephesians 4:20-32*<br>A Source of Comfort<br>What Causes Difference of Vision<br>Nothing But Free Will | November 19th |
| Lesson 9 | *Colossians 3:12-25*<br>Divine in the Beginning<br>Blessings of Contentment<br>Free and Untrammeled Energy | November 26th |
| Lesson 10 | *James 1*<br>The Highest Doctrine<br>A Mantle of Darkness<br>The Counsel of God<br>Blessed Beyond Speaking | December 3rd |
| Lesson 11 | *I Peter 1*<br>Message to the Elect<br>Not of the World's Good | December 10th |
| Lesson 12 | *Revelation 1:9*<br>Self-Glorification<br>The All-Powerful Name<br>Message to the Seven Churches<br>The Voice of the Spirit | December 17th |
| Lesson 13 | Golden Text<br>Responding Principle Lives<br>Principle Not Hidebound<br>They Were Not Free Minded | December 24th |
| Lesson 14 | Review<br>It is Never Too Late<br>The Just Live by Faith<br>An Eternal Offer<br>Freedom of Christian Science | December 31st |

## *Eleventh Series*

### January 1 – March 25, 1894

| | | |
|---|---|---|
| Lesson 1 | *Genesis 1:26-31 & 2:1-3* | January 7th |
| | The First Adam | |
| | Man: The Image of Language Paul and Elymas | |
| Lesson 2 | *Genesis 3:1-15* | January 14th |
| | Adam's Sin and God's Grace | |
| | The Fable of the Garden | |
| | Looked-for Sympathy | |
| | The True Doctrine | |
| Lesson 3 | *Genesis 4:3-13* | January 21st |
| | Types of the Race | |
| | God in the Murderer | |
| | God Nature Unalterable | |
| Lesson 4 | *Genesis 9:8-17* | January 28th |
| | God's Covenant With Noah | |
| | Value of Instantaneous Action | |
| | The Lesson of the Rainbow | |
| Lesson 5 | I Corinthians 8:1-13 | February 4th |
| | *Genesis 12:1-9* | |
| | Beginning of the Hebrew Nation | |
| | No Use For Other Themes | |
| | Influence of Noble Themes | |
| | Danger In Looking Back | |
| Lesson 6 | *Genesis 17:1-9* | February 11th |
| | God's Covenant With Abram | |
| | As Little Children | |
| | God and Mammon | |
| | Being Honest With Self | |
| Lesson 7 | *Genesis 18:22-23* | February 18th |
| | God's Judgment of Sodom | |
| | No Right Nor Wrong In Truth | |
| | Misery Shall Cease | |
| Lesson 8 | *Genesis 22:1-13* | February 25th |
| | Trial of Abraham's Faith | |
| | Light Comes With Preaching | |
| | You Can Be Happy NOW | |

| | | |
|---|---|---|
| Lesson 9 | *Genesis 25:27-34* | March 4th |
| | Selling the Birthright | |
| | "Ye shall be Filled" | |
| | The Delusion Destroyed | |
| Lesson 10 | *Genesis 28:10-22* | March 11th |
| | Jacob at Bethel | |
| | Many Who Act Like Jacob | |
| | How to Seek Inspiration | |
| | Christ, the True Pulpit Orator | |
| | The Priceless Knowledge of God | |
| Lesson 11 | *Proverbs 20:1-7* | March 18th |
| | Temperance | |
| | Only One Lord | |
| | What King Alcohol Does | |
| | Stupefying Ideas | |
| Lesson 12 | *Mark 16:1-8* | March 25th |
| | Review and Easter | |
| | Words of Spirit and Life | |
| | Facing the Supreme | |
| | Erasure of the Law | |
| | Need No Other Friend | |

## Twelfth Series

### April 1 – June 24, 1894

| | | |
|---|---|---|
| Lesson 1 | *Genesis 24:30, 32:09-12* | April 8th |
| | Jacob's Prevailing Prayer | |
| | God Transcends Idea | |
| | All To Become Spiritual | |
| | Ideas Opposed to Each Other | April 1st |
| Lesson 2 | *Genesis 37:1-11* | |
| | Discord in Jacob's Family | |
| | Setting Aside Limitations | |
| | On the Side of Truth | |
| Lesson 3 | *Genesis 37:23-36* | April 15th |
| | Joseph Sold into Egypt | |
| | Influence on the Mind | |
| | Of Spiritual Origin | |
| Lesson 4 | *Genesis 41:38-48* | April 22nd |
| | Object Lesson Presented in | |
| | the Book of Genesis | |
| Lesson 5 | *Genesis 45:1-15* | April 29th |
| | "With Thee is Fullness of Joy" | |
| | India Favors Philosophic Thought | |
| | What These Figures Impart | |
| | The Errors of Governments | |
| Lesson 6 | *Genesis 50:14-26* | May 6th |
| | Changes of Heart | |
| | The Number Fourteen | |
| | Divine Magicians | |
| Lesson 7 | *Exodus 1:1-14* | May 13th |
| | Principle of Opposites | |
| | Power of Sentiment | |
| | Opposition Must Enlarge | |
| Lesson 8 | *Exodus 2:1-10* | May 20th |
| | How New Fires Are Enkindled | |
| | Truth Is Restless | |
| | Man Started from God | |
| Lesson 9 | *Exodus 3:10-20* | May 27th |
| | What Science Proves | |
| | What Today's Lesson Teaches | |
| | The Safety of Moses | |

| | | |
|---|---|---|
| Lesson 10 | *Exodus 12:1-14* | June 3rd |
| | The Exodus a Valuable Force | |
| | What the Unblemished Lamp Typifies | |
| | Sacrifice Always Costly | |
| Lesson 11 | *Exodus 14:19-29* | June 10th |
| | Aristides and Luther Contrasted | |
| | The Error of the Egyptians | |
| | The Christian Life not Easy | |
| | The True Light Explained | |
| Lesson 12 | *Proverbs 23:29-35* | June 17th |
| | Heaven and Christ will Help | |
| | The Woes of the Drunkard | |
| | The Fight Still Continues | |
| | The Society of Friends | |
| Lesson 13 | *Proverbs 23:29-35* | June 24th |
| | Review | |
| | Where is Man's Dominion | |
| | Wrestling of Jacob | |
| | When the Man is Seen | |

# Thirteenth Series

## July 1 – September 30, 1894

| | | |
|---|---|---|
| Lesson 1 | The Birth of Jesus | July 1st |
| | *Luke 2:1-16* | |
| | No Room for Jesus | |
| | Man's Mystic Center | |
| | They glorify their Performances | |
| Lesson 2 | Presentation in the Temple | July 8th |
| | *Luke 2:25-38* | |
| | A Light for Every Man | |
| | All Things Are Revealed | |
| | The Coming Power | |
| | Like the Noonday Sun | |
| Lesson 3 | Visit of the Wise Men | July 15th |
| | *Matthew 1:2-12* | |
| | The Law Our Teacher | |
| | Take neither Scrip nor Purse | |
| | The Star in the East | |
| | The Influence of Truth | |
| Lesson 4 | Flight Into Egypt | July 22nd |
| | *Mathew 2:13-23* | |
| | The Magic Word of Wage Earning | |
| | How Knowledge Affect the Times | |
| | The Awakening of the Common People | |
| Lesson 5 | The Youth of Jesus | July 29th |
| | *Luke2:40-52* | |
| | Your Righteousness is as filthy Rags | |
| | Whatsoever Ye Search, that will Ye Find | |
| | The starting Point of All Men | |
| | Equal Division, the Lesson Taught by Jesus | |
| | The True Heart Never Falters | |
| Lesson 6 | The "All is God" Doctrine | August 5th |
| | *Luke 2:40-52* | |
| | Three Designated Stages of Spiritual Science | |
| | Christ Alone Gives Freedom | |
| | The Great Leaders of Strikes | |
| Lesson 7 | Missing | August 12th |
| Lesson 8 | First Disciples of Jesus | August 19th |
| | *John 1:36-49* | |
| | The Meaning of Repentance | |

|  |  |  |
|---|---|---|
|  | Erase the Instructed Mind | |
|  | The Necessity of Rest | |
|  | The Self-Center No Haltered Joseph | |
| Lesson 9 | The First Miracle of Jesus | August 26th |
|  | *John 2:1-11* | |
|  | "I Myself am Heaven or Hell" | |
|  | The Satan Jesus Recognized | |
|  | The Rest of the People of God | |
|  | John the Beholder of Jesus | |
|  | The Wind of the Spirit | |
| Lesson 10 | Jesus Cleansing the Temple | September 2nd |
|  | *John 2:13-25* | |
|  | The Secret of Fearlessness | |
|  | Jerusalem the Symbol of Indestructible Principle | |
|  | What is Required of the Teacher | |
|  | The Whip of Soft Cords | |
| Lesson 11 | Jesus and Nicodemus | September 9th |
|  | *John 3:1-16* | |
|  | Metaphysical Teaching of Jesus | |
|  | Birth-Given Right of Equality | |
|  | Work of the Heavenly Teacher | |
| Lesson 12 | Jesus at Jacob's Well | September 16th |
|  | *John 4:9-26* | |
|  | The Question of the Ages | |
|  | The Great Teacher and Healer | |
|  | "Because I Live, Ye shall Live Also." | |
|  | The Faith That is Needful | |
| Lesson 13 | Daniel's Abstinence | September 23rd |
|  | *Daniel 1:8-20* | |
|  | Knowledge is Not All | |
|  | Between the Oriental and Occidental Minds | |
|  | The Four Servants of God | |
|  | The Saving Power of Good | |
|  | The Meeting-Ground of Spirit and Truth | |
| Lesson 14 | Take With You Words | September 30th |
|  | *John 2:13-25* | |
| Review | Healing Comes from Within | |
|  | The Marthas and Marys of Christianity | |
|  | The Summing up of The Golden Texts | |

# Fourteenth Series

## October 7 – December 30, 1894

| | | |
|---|---|---|
| Lesson 1 | Jesus At Nazareth | October 7th |
| *Luke 4:16-30* | Jesus Teaches Uprightness | |
| | The Pompous Claim of a Teacher | |
| | The Supreme One No Respecter of Persons | |
| | The Great Awakening | |
| | The Glory of God Will Come Back | |
| Lesson 2 | The Draught of Fishes | October 14th |
| *Luke 5:1-11* | The Protestant Within Every Man | |
| | The Cry of Those Who Suffer | |
| | Where the Living Christ is Found | |
| Lesson 3 | The Sabbath in Capernaum | October 21st |
| *Mark 1:21-34* | Why Martyrdom Has Been a Possibility | |
| | The Truth Inculcated in Today's Lesson | |
| | The Injustice of Vicarious Suffering | |
| | The Promise of Good Held in the Future | |
| Lesson 4 | The Paralytic Healed | October 28th |
| *Mark 2:1-12* | System Of Religions and Philosophy | |
| | The Principle Of Equalization | |
| | The Little Rift In School Methods | |
| | What Self-Knowledge Will Bring | |
| | The Meaning Of The Story of Capernaum | |
| Lesson 5 | Reading of Sacred Books | November 4th |
| *Mark 2:23-38* | The Interior Qualities | |
| *Mark 2:1-4* | The Indwelling God | |
| | Weakness Of The Flesh | |
| | The Unfound Spring | |
| Lesson 6 | Spiritual Executiveness | November 11th |
| *Mark 3:6-19* | The Teaching Of The Soul | |
| | The Executive Powers Of The Mind | |
| | Vanity Of Discrimination | |
| | Truth Cannot Be Bought Off | |
| | And Christ Was Still | |
| | The Same Effects For Right And Wrong | |
| | The Unrecognized Splendor Of The Soul | |

| | | |
|---|---|---|
| Lesson 7 | Twelve Powers Of The Soul | November 18th |
| *Luke 6:20-31* | The Divine Ego in Every One | |
| | Spiritual Better than Material Wealth | |
| | The Fallacy Of Rebuke | |
| | Andrew, The Unchanging One | |
| Lesson 8 | Things Not Understood Attributed to Satan | |
| *Mark 3:22-35* | True Meaning Of Hatha Yoga | November 25th |
| | The Superhuman Power Within Man | |
| | The Problem of Living and Prospering | |
| | Suffering Not Ordained for Good | |
| | The Lamb in the Midst shall Lead | |
| Lesson 9 | Independence of Mind | December 2nd |
| *Luke 7:24-35* | He that Knoweth Himself Is Enlightened | |
| | The Universal Passion for Saving Souls | |
| | Strength From knowledge of Self | |
| | Effect Of Mentally Directed Blows | |
| Lesson 10 | The Gift of Untaught wisdom | December 9th |
| *Luke 8:4-15* | The Secret Of Good Comradeship | |
| | The Knower That Stands in Everyone | |
| | Laying Down the Symbols | |
| | Intellect The Devil Which Misleads | |
| | Interpretation Of The Day's Lesson | |
| Lesson 11 | The Divine Eye Within | December 16th |
| *Matthew 5:5-16* | Knowledge Which Prevails Over Civilization | |
| | The Message Heard By Matthew | |
| | The Note Which shatters Walls Of Flesh | |
| Lesson 12 | Unto Us a Child I s Born | December 23rd |
| *Luke 7:24-35* | The Light That is Within | |
| | Significance Of The Vision of Isaiah | |
| | Signs of the Times | |
| | The New Born Story Of God | |
| | Immaculate Vision Impossible To None | |
| Lesson 13 | Review | December 30th |
| *Isaiah 9:2-7* | That Which Will Be Found In The Kingdom | |
| | Situation Of Time And Religion Reviewed | |
| | Plea That Judgment May Be Righteous | |
| | The Souls Of All One And Changeless | |

www.ingramcontent.com/pod-product-compliance
Lightning Source LLC
Chambersburg PA
CBHW060656100426
42734CB00047B/1948